W9-CHB-050

DATE DUE

JAN 1 5 1997	
FEB 1 0 2001	
JUN 0 1 2006	

BRODART   Cat. No. 23-221

ETHICS
AND
NATIONAL
DEFENSE

ETHICS
AND
NATIONAL
DEFENSE

THE TIMELESS
ISSUES

EDITED BY
JAMES C. GASTON
AND
JANIS BREN HIETALA

WITHDRAWN

NATIONAL DEFENSE UNIVERSITY PRESS
Washington, D.C.

U 22 .EB3 1993

Ethics and national defense

AQQ4271-8/1

National Defense University Press Publications. To increase general knowledge and inform discussion, NDU Press publishes books on subjects relating to U.S. national security. Each year, in this effort, the National Defense University, through the Institute for National Strategic Studies, hosts about two dozen Senior Fellows who engage in original research on national security issues. NDU Press publishes the best of this research. In addition, the Press publishes especially timely or distinguished writing on national security from authors outside the University, new editions of out-of-print defense classics, and books based on conferences concerning national security affairs.

This publication is not copyrighted and may be quoted or reprinted without permission. Please give full publication credit.

Opinions, conclusions, and recommendations expressed or implied within are solely those of the authors and do not necessarily represent the views of the National Defense University, the Department of Defense, or any other Government agency.

Proofread by Mary Close, NDU Press writer-editor. Indexed by SSR, Inc., Washington, DC.

NDU Press publications are sold by the U.S. Government Printing Office. For ordering information, call (202) 783-3238, or write to: Superintendent of Documents, U.S. Government Printing Office, Washington, D.C. 20402.

GPO Stock No. 008-020-01262-9

ISBN 0-16-035907-4

Library of Congress Cataloging-in-Publication Data

Ethics and national defense : the timeless issues / edited by James C.
  Gaston and Janis Bren Hietala.
      p.   cm.
    Includes bibliographical references and index.
    1. Military ethics. I. Gaston, James C. II. Hietala, Janis
  Bren.
U22.E83 1993   92-43194
174'.9355—dc20   CIP

First printing, February 1993

RECEIVED

NOV 0 1993

Kennedy School
Library

CONTENTS

PART I
ETHICAL FOUNDATIONS OF MILITARY SERVICE

These essays deal with fundamental issues of profound significance to all service members. They address the very core of what it means to perform military service for one's country.

PART II
PROFESSIONS WITHIN A PROFESSION

These essays come out of issues in the fields of law, medicine, and intelligence to consider ethical relationships among those professions and the military. Examining military ethics from the viewpoints of other professions, the

authors provide valuable insights into ethical issues faced by
all service members.

PART III
TRAINING FOR ETHICAL BEHAVIOR
IN THE ARMED FORCES

These essays cover both the difficulties and the importance
of ethics instruction. They also point the way toward effective instruction with both general and specific guidelines for
successful programs.

PART IV
CONTEMPORARY ISSUES IN MILITARY ETHICS

The essays examine controversial issues that figure promi-
nently in discussions of contemporary military ethics. They
look closely at the ethical dimensions of the Strategic Defense Initiative, American involvement in small wars, and
combat assignments for women. In each case, the author
analyzes central issues and defines a favored position.

CONTENTS

FOREWORD

The National Defense University has, for many years, cosponsored the Joint Services Conference on Professional Ethics (JSCOPE) to contribute to the continuing dialogue on ethical issues. At this annual forum, representatives of the military, academic, and policy communities discuss the most troubling ethical issues that confront the profession of arms. Recent conferences have examined such matters as the conduct of the Vietnam war, procurement scandals, and problems accompanying the changing demographics of the armed services. The discussions cross service lines into the joint arena, making them especially appropriate as the US military prepares to meet the regional challenges of the 1990s.

This volume of essays, selected from recent JSCOPE conferences, is rooted in the belief that discussion of ethical matters is an appropriate and important pursuit for military officers. These essays specifically address the ethical traditions of the profession of arms, the potential conflict of overlapping professional obligations when doctors and lawyers don military uniforms, how the armed services teach ethics, and the question of women in combat roles.

The post-Cold War world, wherein shades of gray are replacing the blacks and whites of superpower competition, promises to make ethical inquiry more subtle and complex. To paraphrase the British military leader Sir James Glover, however, in a free society the soldier who functions best is the soldier who is guided by a quiet but active conscience.

PAUL G. CERJAN
LIEUTENANT GENERAL, U.S. ARMY
PRESIDENT, NATIONAL DEFENSE UNIVERSITY

PART I

ETHICAL FOUNDATIONS OF MILITARY SERVICE

᭲᭲᭲

SPECIAL TRUST AND CONFIDENCE

THOMAS J. BEGINES
Captain, U.S. Army

Captain Begines examines possible sources for the "special trust and confidence" which the president reposes in military officers. Conventional notions of patriotism, valor, and fidelity prove inadequate, according to Begines, and only the deeply personal moral autonomy of each officer remains to merit trust and confidence.

To anyone who has ever attended an appointment or promotion ceremony for an officer in the Armed Forces the words *special trust and confidence* are familiar ones. At such times we are reminded that the responsibility of the American military officer is to be worthy of special trust and confidence. Because of the importance and fundamental nature of that common charge, officers should ideally have a clear understanding of what it is that they have been tasked to do, yet the exact nature of that charge is not immediately apparent. If pressed to explain this charge, most officers would probably first attempt to place the phrase in the context of promotion orders of the *Officer's Guide*. "The President of the United States has reposed special trust and confidence in the patriotism, valor, fidelity, and abilities of [the officer being promoted]." But how are we to perceive each of those "bedrock" attributes we have been charged with "special trust and confidence" to initiate and promote?

Some officers no doubt view patriotism in a somewhat chauvinistic sense—military officers are to physically defend the people and territories of the United States. Their patriotism resides in a professional ethic requiring the officer to fight ably to achieve the military goals that have been assigned. Much as a lawyer is professionally committed to providing the best defense possible for his client, regardless of the guilt or innocence of that client, a truly patriotic officer will set aside any individual judgment he might have about the moral worth of the mission assigned and will do his best to accomplish that mission—"my country, right or wrong."[1] Indeed, despite having been relieved for opposing the policies of his civilian superiors, General MacArthur, in his celebrated address at West Point in 1962, counseled just such a view:

> Others will debate the controversial issues, national and international, which divide men's minds. But serene, calm, aloof, you stand as the Nation's war guardian. . . . These great national problems are not for your professional participation or military solution.

But even as comfort is taken in the belief that in the adversarial system of jurisprudence the guilty will not usually win their case, in some instances the truly guilty do prevail. In a strong sense, people feel this to be fundamentally unjust and immoral. Despite professional ethics, we fault the defense lawyer for his complicity in allowing, indeed abetting, one in the wrong to prevail. Analogously, some military officers may take utilitarian comfort in the assumption that when they are ordered to inflict violence or to refrain from inflicting violence the nation will usually have just cause. Some officers believe that a professional ethic absolves them of responsibility for defending (successfully) an unjust cause. However, other officers view this nonjudgmental "hired gun" conception of patriotism as wrong. These officers see an inescapably moral component to patriotism. They believe they are acting patriotically only when, by their words and actions, they pursue policies and decisions that they believe truly promote "the American way of life." If they perceive a policy or decision to be wrong in the sense of being practically or morally harmful to the American way of life, these officers believe it is their "special trust and confidence" to act against or around those policies and decisions. General MacArthur, General Singlaub, and Lieutenant Colonel North have all claimed to be patriots in precisely this regard.

How can anyone understand *valor*? Some officers might conceive the concept simply as an expectation that they will be physically courageous on the battlefield. Other officers might understand valor as possessing the moral courage in their professional actions. The term *fidelity* is likewise deeply ambiguous. Are soldiers to understand fidelity as loyalty to the chain-of-command or to the members of the unit or to achieving the mission or to oneself, realizing that all these concerns are hoped to be mutually achievable but are not necessarily so? Some officers may understand fidelity in the sense (apparent) of the Marine Corps motto "Semper Fidelis," namely, to be true to the function of the Armed Forces and maintain selves and units in a high state of psychological and physical readiness to win the wars of this nation. Thus far, an interim conclusion about the meaning of the phrase "special trust and confidence" in the context of officer appointment or promotion orders yields deeply ambiguous results. This avenue of inquiry does not help us to clearly understand our "marching orders."

* * *

Perhaps the responsibilities of "special trust and confidence" can be illuminated by examining a written delineation more fundamental than promotion orders, namely, the oath of office of military officers. Upon commissioning, every officer gives express consent to a contract, wherein he or she swears to

> support and defend the Constitution of the United States against all enemies, foreign and domestic, [and to] bear true faith and allegiance to the same [Constitution].

This special trust and confidence is to support the tenets of the U.S. Constitution. However, this approach fails to yield clear or adequate guidance.

First, merely note the deep and continuing disagreement concerning the nature and the normative limits of consent, even explicit consent, and the whole note of contractarianism.[2] Many objections focus upon what some see as inherent vagueness or ambiguity in the notion of consent. Regarding limits, for example, many have argued that one simply cannot contract to do some things (for example, acts that violate moral autonomy [enslave you] or compel to do inherently immoral things).

It is also an unwarranted generalization to assert that most military officers have, at best, an incomplete knowledge of the Constitution or, at worst, a sketchy or distorted understanding of the tenets of that document.[3] Officers are not unaware of the limits of their military authority or of the functions of their office, both of which are (somewhat) circumscribed by the Constitution, but most officers do not consciously ground their moral decisions in the tenets of the Constitution. A fortiori, it is not even possible to adequately correct this epistemic failure.

The Constitution is not a complete or finished product but an incomplete and evolving body of law and underlying moral precepts. It is the business of individuals (the Supreme Court), ostensibly our most learned lawyers, to divine the intent of the framers and to resolve apparent conflicts within "the law of the land." Military officers could not perform these interpretations.[4]

It is counterintuitive to assert that officers make their moral judgments, particularly those made on the battlefield, by appealing to their oath of office. For these reasons, an attempt to ground the "special trust and confidence" of the officer in the oath of office, and ultimately in the Constitution, furnishes inadequate guidance.

* * *

A possible approach to explaining adequately the concept of special trust and confidence asserts that an officer's ultimate responsibility is to defend the national interests. Many officers view their responsibility in just such practical, "concrete" terms. These officers construe their obligation to be the preservation of territorial integrity and political sovereignty or, alternately, to the preservation of our capacity for continued self-determination. In yet more definitive terms, the obligation is to achieve and protect the conditions that make existence as an independent people possible—the retention of natural assets for use, the safe-guarding of oil supplies, waterways, essential commercial ventures, spheres of influence, etc. Yet there is nothing in this essentially "Reasons of State" doctrine that is specifically American or moral.

Many officers would insist that there is a value-laden component to their obligation. These officers see *their* special trust and confidence to be the protection (to use an expression of Walzer's) of "our common [American] way of life." More specifically, this encompasses the defense of American *values* as well as the defense of American assets, a seemingly indeterminable task to definitively and exhaustively make specific. Officers embracing a value-laden conception of "our national interest" might well view their participation in a chauvinistic use of American military power as itself immoral. One rhetorical question will serve to adequately illustrate the contention that the notion of "national interests" is deeply ambiguous: "Did our participation in and conduct of the war in Vietnam truly promote our national interests?"

* * *

Attempts to ground adequately the special trust and confidence of the officer in the attributes recognized in promotion ceremonies, in the oath of office, and in a concept of serving the national interests are all seriously flawed. Summarized, these flaws are pernicious vagueness or ambiguity which permits undesirable interpretations or incompleteness (that is, a lack of adequate guidance for decision making) or simple unfamiliarity. Explaining the last flaw more fully points the way to a solution.

E. M. Adams has argued persuasively that all well-formed senses of responsibility rest upon and are in harmony with the fundamental personhood, "the constitutive responsibility of which is to define and to live a life of one's own that will pass muster under rational and moral criticism." This means that we fulfill our responsibilities as persons only when attempting to do what is believed morally and rationally right personally. A person forms a world view and an understanding of himself as an individual moral agent in that world. As a moral agent the person has a continuing need to make moral decisions which satisfy him as a rational individual. Hence, people place a two-fold responsibility upon themselves. First, personal morality must be complete enough, familiar enough, and persuasive enough (to each) to actually imbue personal decisions. Second, people must decide and act with consistency and conviction. Each moral decision must be integrated with all of the significant moral decisions previously made throughout a lifetime.

Because of these requirements, no significant vagueness or ambiguity or unfamiliarity can really be said to exist in personal morality. This is not to say that people always act in accordance with their personal moral principles (the ancient problem of akrasia) or that their personal morality is more fundamental than social morality.

One immediate objection to the belief advanced that personal morality must be viewed as more fundamental than social morality, even in the fulfillment of a social office, is the well-founded contention that people can only achieve a meaningful, significant personal morality after exposure to social mores. This view is not contested.[5] After people have formed a personal morality, this personal morality is more familiar, more complete, and ultimately more compelling than any social morality entailed by any particular social office.

The ubiquitous, transcending, and unifying notion present within the American Constitution and the American way of life is the primacy people have traditionally afforded moral autonomy. Although the public faults individuals for affirming moral stances believed to be based upon insufficiently good or insincere reasons and acts to prevent individuals, however sincere, from causing harm to others without just cause, people nonetheless treat individuals who "break the rules" or "buck the system" for what they see as compelling moral reasons with a certain amount of tolerance, respect, and leniency in most walks of American life. The motivating notion seems to be that individual moral dissent ought to be tolerated as a safeguard against institutional injustices or immoralities.

Bearing all this in mind, perhaps an officer's special trust and confidence ought to be based upon a single expectation and requirement: that the officer will maintain moral autonomy. In other words, an officer's special trust and confidence is that the officer will not violate personal moral convictions in the fulfillment of official responsibilities. Affirming such a stance requires that the military tolerate some instances of moral dissent within the ranks.

The notion of tolerating moral dissent within the ranks is antithetical to what Samuel P. Huntington called "the supreme military value of obedience." (Huntington was making a descriptive, empirical claim and not a prescriptive, normative claim.) Closely allied to this military notion of the virtues of unfailing obedience is the notion that self-sacrifice must always be considered a virtuous trait. As an instructor of moral philosophy at a military academy, when I place cadets into hypothetical battlefield situations, I often encounter a disturbing belief born of a misconception of the virtues of obedience and self-sacrifice. I believe this is a misconception that is shared, regrettably, by a number of serving officers. The ill-founded belief is that officers are *required* at times to do things that they believe to be intrinsically immoral, that is, which their personal morality forbids, in order to achieve the "high duty" of their official responsibility—to "accomplish the mission" or to "spare their soldiers." For example, many cadets say that even though they would feel a deontological constraint and "personally" think it was wrong to torture a prisoner to gain vital information, they feel they are *required* by their role to sacrifice their selfish desire for "moral purity" in order to reduce the risk of death or wounding of their soldiers or to get the mission accomplished. The rebuttal is two-fold.

If people are serious about a moral dimension to officership, it is deeply inconsistent to claim to be maintaining or promoting American values while violating those same values. If people sanction the notion that at any time there is a requirement for a "disappearing moral self," they place themselves on a slippery slope with utter realism at the bottom and echo the hollow "orders are orders" defense of Nuremberg. Hence, a first caveat is that people ought not to tolerate official conduct based upon a personal "morality" of realism (that is, actions guided by the belief that military violence is not subject to moral constraints).

As a second caveat, an officer's personal morality cannot be one of strict pacifism. It is an obvious and specific function of a military officer to be morally and practically prepared to inflict and manage significant violence or to support those efforts. To assume that responsibility while asserting a personal morality of pacifism is simply unconscionable.[6]

A personal morality of ethical egoism, even enlightened egoism, is incompatible with the role of the military officer because an officer is required to act for "the common good," the vague but clearly collective "national interests," and "the welfare of the soldiers."

It is a necessary requirement for the officer to act within at least one rule-utilitarian restriction to preserve the form and stability of our society; any decisive moral dissent must occur only within the ranks of the military and not contravene the decisions of the civil authorities. In other words, this does not say that an officer, after dissenting, must ultimately still obey orders which he or she believes to be immoral. An officer in such situations may resign or refuse to obey the order but ought not to take positive actions contrary to a superior's orders.[7]

Despite the caveats upon acceptable personal moralities vis-a-vis the proper fulfillment of the social office of military officer, this presents an essentially libertarian view. I believe we should resist the stipulation of directed or universal moral requirements of this social office which are significantly more stringent than the ones I have given. We should require our officers to be reflective about moral matters. In our military schools and institutions, we should discursively teach moral theory and delineate certain personal moralities (my caveats) as incompatible with our social office (responsible role). However, we ought not to promote a professional ethic which is an exhaustive and overriding set of specific values. Such stipulations are likely to be poorly conceived or misconceived by the individual. Such stipulations do violence to the concept of the primacy of individual moral autonomy, a concept which I argue is the guiding tenet and raison d'etre of "the American way of life." If we are truly serious about the moral component of our social office, we must embrace a conception of special trust and confidence that requires and permits morally based dissent within the bounds I describe.

NOTES

1. Colonel Dennis Coupe, U.S. Army War College, brought to my attention "new model rules" being proposed for Staff Judge Advocates that would obligate military lawyers not just to

assure procedural justice but, in some cases, to help promote substantive justice as well.

2. See, for example, Hanna Pitkin, "Obligation and Consent—I," *American Political Science Review* 59 (December 1965); A. John Simmons, *Moral Principles and Political Obligations* (Princeton, NJ: Princeton University Press, 1979); J.P. Plamenatz, *Consent, Freedom, and Political Obligation*, 2nd ed. (London: Oxford, 1968).

3. I owe this insight to a conversation I had with Major Gary Coleman, Department of English, U.S. Military Academy, in September 1988.

4. For example, as Major Gary Coleman pointed out in "The Constitution as Moral Guide," a paper presented at the Joint Academy Conference on Constitutional Responsibilities, January 11, 1989, in Washington, DC, the textbook on constitutional law used at the U.S. Military Academy explains six separate approaches to interpreting the Constitution. His paper contains a number of other insights into difficulties associated with interpreting the Constitution.

5. I am grateful to Major Wayne Mastin, U.S. Military Academy, for reminding me of this notion. I believe that it can be well substantiated by a digression into state of nature arguments, themselves apparently grounded in the ancient Greek concept of autarkeia. See, for example, Charles Taylor, "Atomism," in *Powers, Possessions, and Freedoms: Essays in Honor of C. B. Macpherson*, ed. Alkis Kontos (Toronto University Press, 1979), p. 41.

6. Obviously, this restriction need not apply to certain military personnel, such as doctors.

7. My thanks to Captain Jeff Whitman for pointing out the need for this clarification.

BIBLIOGRAPHY

Adams, E. Maynard. "Human Rights and the Social Order." *The Journal of Value Inquiry* 22 (1988): 167-81.

Crocker, Lawrence P., ed. *Army Officer's Guide*. Harrisburg, PA: Stackpole Books, 1983.

Coleman, Gary. "The Political Responsibilities of Army Office." Unpublished paper, U.S. Military Academy at West Point, NY, 1987.

Huntington, Samuel P. "The Military Mind: Conservative Realism of the Professional Military Ethic." In *War, Morality, and the Military Profession*, pp. 25-49. Edited by Malham M. Wakin. Boulder, CO: Westview Press, 1979.

MacArthur, Douglas. "Duty, Honor, Country." Speech delivered to the Corps of Cadets and select members of the faculty at the U.S. Military Academy, West Point, New York, 12 May 1962. Printed in Department of Defense Pamphlet GEN-1. *Duty, Honor, Country*. Washington, DC: U.S. Government Printing Office, 1962. (0-647457)

Walzer, Michael. *Just and Unjust Wars*. New York: Basic Books, 1977.

⁓⧽) ⧼⁓

THE OFFICER'S OATH:
WORDS THAT BIND

JAMES H. McGRATH
Central Michigan University

Professor McGrath's concern is with the meaning of the oath taken by officers when they agree to accept the "special trust and confidence" of the president. Surveying the meanings of similar oaths in history, McGrath focuses a new light on this oath as a voluntary, public vow by which one consents to be bound by others.

I was breaking into a cold sweat . . . I was being solicited to entice my junior officers to betray their oath of office, their Code of Conduct, their country.
—A DISTINGUISHED POW'S AUTOBIOGRAPHY

You have held personal safety and comfort above duty, honor, and country, and, in so doing, have deliberately violated your oath as a citizen of the United States and as an officer of the United States Army.
—A POW REPRIMAND ORDER

In the midst of a time when the American officer corps was being told that it had lost its ethical bearing, James Webb, the former Secretary of the Navy, advised us to grab a piece of traditional "flotsam" when we are ethically adrift. Is the comissioned officer's oath essential military cargo or is it merely baggage the profession would be no worse off jettisoning?

The commissioned officer's oath does carry an impressive resumé. Today's officers take the same oath that officers have taken since 1884. As early as 1634, our forefathers pledged to be "true and faithful" to the government of the commonwealth. The very first item printed on a printing press in the American colonies was an oath. George Washington crusaded for an oath, and today's officers are required by the Constitution to take one.

But is this resumé like the bathing suit that reveals a lot that is interesting while hiding what is important? Oaths seems to be born of a suspicion hardly befitting special trust and confidence; "civil blackmail," Kant called it. Historically, oaths are rooted in the magic of a self-imposed curse. When they have divine sanctions they are unnecessary. When they do not, they are ineffective. And what of that one "fixed star in our consitutional constellation?" Justice Jackson wrote in *West Virginia v. Barnett* that "no official, high or petty, can prescribe what shall be orthodox in politics, nationalism, religion, or other matters of opinion."

With the oath's historical context in mind, I propose answers to three questions about the commissioned officer's oath. These answers suggest that the profession has an opportunity to reaffirm the oath as a professional resource, a piece of traditional flotsam.

Question: When I take my oath, *what* do I solemnly swear *to do*?

It is a mistake to think that the function of the oath is to establish something important that commissioned officers have a sworn obligation to do.[1] The oath contains only three clauses that are sources of sworn obligations. However, none of the clauses is the source of a significant, distinctive, definite, officer's obligation.

An officer swears "to bear true faith and allegiance to the" Constitution. Yet, if he was a naturalized citizen when he took his oath, he already had that sworn obligation; the naturalization oath set out in our Immigration and Naturalization Act contains a verbatim "bear allegiance" clause. The obligation would be new only for a citizen by birth who rejected the view that his citizenship itself provides an allegiance obligation. Moreover, for American officers who have simply accepted the civilian-military subordination without "giving the Constitution a second thought", the obligation has been no more significant for them than it has been for their European forefathers who, in the last two hundred years, have faced decisions of continued allegiance only at a few "rare critical moments."[2]

An officer has a sworn obligation to "support and defend the Constitution." But what is that obligation? Is it the same obligation that arises from the same "support and defend" clause of the naturalization oath? Is an officer's obligation to defend "against all enemies, foreign and domestic" the same as the obligation of the FBI agent who takes an identical oath? Is the officer's obligation the same as the one the verbatim "support and defend" clause of the enlisted oath provides?

These two Constitution clauses are unlikely to be very definite for the officer on the ground or in the cockpit. Even the cognoscenti—Sir John Hackett, Morris Janowitz, Richard Gabriel, and Thomas Reese—dispute the object of allegiance: Is it to the Constitution's text? to its latest interpretation? to its underlying values? or to the position or to the person of commander-in-chief?

An officer swears in the oath's third clause to "discharge the duties of his office." But this clause also provides no distinctive sworn obligations. The U.S. Code requires members of the Postal Service and Peace Corps volunteers, as well as officers, to take the same oath. One duty clause cannot be the source of three distinctly different duties attendant to three different offices.

The practice of appealing to the oath to determine an officer's sworn obligations overlooks the critical fact that the text we have been examining becomes a commissioned officer's oath (rather than a naturalization, FBI, enlisted, or Peace Corps oath) only after "the *duties* of *the office* upon which *I* am about to enter" have been specified.[3]

That specification stems from the officer's commission which charges an officer to "discharge the duties of [his] office . . . by doing and performing all manner of things . . . during the pleasure of the President." The only way to know how the three-clause oath becomes a commissioned officer's oath is to know what those "things" are. Only then can we know what an officer swears to do when he takes his oath.

The shape of those "all manner of things," to adapt an evocative image, is an inverted triangle with fuzzy edges. The text of the oath alone does little more than place such sworn obligations as those "to render unconditional obedience to Adolph Hitler" or "to be devoted to my last breath to my Soviet motherland" outside this triangle of an officer's professional duties. An ensign has a glimpse of only the triangle's tip. It may provide something like a sketch of a dramatic part awaiting him. So when that ensign reports that he has "no idea what it really means to be a naval officer," we admire his candor and honesty. Commanders and captains see enough of the triangle to dispute public policy responsibilities. They disagree because, from start to finish, the edges of the triangle remain fuzzy.[4]

When an officer takes his oath *what* does he swear *to do*? What are his sworn obligations? The answer: He swears to "discharge the duties of [his] office by doing . . . all manner of things . . . during the pleasure of the President" or until he resigns his commission.

The professional value of the oath is not to be found in the specifications of an officer's obligations. None of these specifications is significant, distinctive, and definite.

Question: When I say "I do solemnly swear that I will," *what* do I *do*?

David Hume's philosophical legacy includes a series of questions that continues to repay serious thought. Hume might have noted that after I say "I do solemnly swear" (in the right circumstances) I then have certain obligations that I did not previously have. But, he would have asked, why do I have those obligations? No stranger to common sense, Hume would have accepted the obvious answer: "simply because I freely uttered those words." Still, he would have persisted, just what is it about saying those words that creates the obligation? Hume considered two options as answers.[5]

The option Hume himself accepted begins with the observation that the swearing of the oath is an essentially social act. On a Humeian account, when I took the oath, I entered into certain relationships with others. Now they can expect me and rely upon me to do certain things. In a word, I promised. A promise, said Hume, is a "human invention, a *certain form of words* . . . by which we bind ourselves to the performance of an action." By promising, I *obligate* myself to some promisee who then holds a *right* of expectation. Because of this right the promisee can *demand*, if necessary, that I do what I have promised to do.

I do not take my oath in an institutional vacuum. With various implicit and explicit promises of its own, the profession also obligates itself to me; it makes me a promisee who also holds certain rights of expectation. On this account, when I say "I do solemnly swear," I exchange mutually conditional promises with my profession. We enter into a contract.[6]

According to Hume's second option, when I say those words an obligation arises from my "mere will and consent." Any social setting or any expectations of others is incidental, and I am bound only by my own solitary consent.

However, Hume rejected the idea that my solitary act of intending to be obligated can actually create an obligation out of thin air. It is a "manifest absurdity" and "may even be compared to *transubstantiation* or *holy orders*," the theological doctrine "whereby a certain form of words, along with a certain intention, changes entirely the nature of a human creature."

I will now propose an answer to the question, "What do I do when I say 'I do solemnly swear'?"

22

that incorporates both of Hume's options. When I *leave* my commissioning ceremony, my social act of swearing has set into motion the machinery of obligations, rights, and demands generated by the promise of Hume's first option. When I *arrive* at my ceremony, I bring something like the solitary "mere will and consent" of Hume's second option. The description of my candidate for this solitary something involves the following three concepts.

Intentions. When I arrive at my commissioning ceremony I bring my intention to become an officer. Intentions can be relatively trivial; for example, I intend to watch the Super Bowl this year. Intentions are also essentially solitary or nonsocial. Although you are now privy to my Super Bowl intention, my intentions are mine and are usually never communicated to anyone else. Every intention also involves some degree of commitment; if my practical life is to take shape, my Super Bowl intention commits me to buy a ticket, not schedule a conflict, etc.

Every intention involves two times. First is that time when I intend to become an officer. There is also that later period of time during which I intend to be an officer—"during the Pleasure."

Vows. I also arrive with a vow to remain an officer. The term *vow* here refers to something less trivial than an intention, but not to anything especially honorific. For example, last year I vowed to stop smoking. Like my Super Bowl intention, my smoking vow is now "out of the bag." Nonetheless, vows are as solitary and nonsocial as intentions. My vows are mine to communicate only if I wish. And even when I do elect to express a vow, I create no vowee.

Every vow includes two intentions. A vow to be an officer includes the mere intention to be an officer. It also includes a second intention not to change (or to impose limits on changing) that first intention. If I now have a vow to be an officer "during the Pleasure," I also now intend not to change my mind "during the Pleasure" about my intention to remain an officer.

With my vows I intend to keep on intending. With a vow comes resolve. I bind myself with my vows. If I vowed last year to quit smoking and I haven't smoked since, it is only a little Pickwickian to say that I have remained loyal or faithful to myself.

(With only the solitary acts of intending and "intending to keep on intending"—vowing—we have already arrived at something resembling "an intention to be bound in conscience to the faithful performance of certain acts," which is how one dictionary defines *oath*.)

Solemn Vows. If my intentions to continue not smoking or to remain an officer are important enough to me, then I bind myself with a vow; I resolve not to change my mind later on about those things. Whenever a resolve to be bound is earnest, sincere, or following from deliberate, serious thought, it is solemn. *Solemn* can refer either to that which is "associated with religious rites" or to that which is "of a serious, grave, or earnest character."

By accepting both of these definitions, we allow that a solemn vow may be either sacred or secular. In either case, the individual appeals to his conscience in his own way. In neither case is a vow solemn because of anything formal, public, or ceremonial.

My candidate for that Humeian solitary something that arises from my "mere will and consent" is my solemn vow.

When I arrive at my commissioning ceremony, I will bring a solemn vow. At the ceremony, I will be offered a commission. I will then take my oath. When I take my oath, I publicly reveal my previously solitary solemn vow. In doing so I make a promise— to "discharge the duties of [my] office . . . by doing . . . all manner of things . . . during the Pleasure of the President" or until I resign my commission.

I arrived with a vow. I left with both a promise and a revealed vow. When I say "I do solemnly that I will," *What* do I *do*? A satisfactory answer must recognize both the oath-as-promise and the oath-as-revealed-vow.

Question: Why do I opt to take my oath?

Some very good answers to this final question are based on the oath-as-promise. Taking the oath does create promises. The swearing is a social act made in a certain institutional context. After I take my oath, others can rely upon me to "discharge the duties of [my] office" so they then issue my first duty station orders. In turn, I can expect to begin drawing second lieutenant's pay. Because I opted to take my oath, I leave my ceremony with a contractual agreement.

But is this the whole story? Any solitary intentions I may have had at the time played no part in that first answer. If those intentions really had no part, the officer's oath would be like a courtroom oath. Consider a witness caught lying under oath. If the witness pleaded for exemption from perjury on the grounds that when he took his oath he did not intend to tell the whole truth—he had his mental fingers crossed—he would be laughed out of court. In a courtroom, all that matters is exactly what Hume said matters: saying the words and creating the expectations.

A second cluster of answers is based on the oath-as-revealed vow. I arrive at my ceremony with a vow and I opt to take the oath in order to reveal that vow. These answers regard the social act of swearing as the revealing of the "mere will and consent" and solitary intent of that vow.

All these revealed-vow answers are anchored in a critical institutional fact once spelled out by Vice Admiral Gerald E. Miller at a change of command ceremony:

> Having been *offered* a commission by virtue of the special trust and confidence which the President has chosen to place in them, these officers have then faced the option of either accepting or rejecting the commission.

Major General Kenneth L. Peek, U.S. Air Force, in a commander's brief, reiterated the same idea in these words:

> Congress confers upon an individual a military officer's commission but the status that accompanies that commission—the honor of serving our Nation as an officer—is gained solely through the individual's acceptance of and commitment to patriotism, valor, abilities, and fidelity.

Because the officer's oath is an *oath of acceptance*, it could not be more wrong to say that the "Federal Government *forces* those who are seeking *employment* (including members of the armed forces) to take an *oath of allegiance.*"[7] The officer's oath is an oath of acceptance, an oath of consent.

The Roman military oath was distinctively an oath of consent to be bound. The Latin term for oath, *sacramentum,* is translated as "engagement" or "the act of binding oneself." With their personal pledges, Romans bound themselves to their commanding generals or legionary standards; in some cases, "soldiers voluntarily took [it] upon themselves" to bind themselves to each other. In each case they also bound themselves to discharge some particular duty: to reassemble, not to quit the ranks, not to steal in camp.

Tertullian was the first theologian to write in Latin and he drew from Roman stoicism. ("Seneca is often one of us.") Therefore, we should not be surprised that he was the first Christian writer to consistently use the (profane) Latin term *sacramentum.* For Tertullian, the Christian sacraments, much like the Roman military oath, include a commitment, allegiance, or engagement and a willingness to accept a new binding relationship. Today, in the definition of *baptism* as "the binding of oneself to Christian doctrine," we encounter the same Roman ideas.

We may or may not follow Hume and dismiss the sacraments of transubstantiation and holy orders as "monstrous doctrines." Still, we have a contemporary, secular counterpart of the Roman military oath which sprang from consent and resulted in a tie that bound with a "cohesive force of incalculable strength."

The French put it best with *se marier avec,* "one marries oneself with someone else" (with a chaplain as witness). To say "I got married by a chaplain" suggests a ceremony different from one in which each person consents to be bound to the other by the revealing of a vow.

The Roman military oath, the concept of the sacraments, and French expression all show that we do "mere(ly) consent" to be bound to others with whom we then stand in certain normative relations. As architects of our own moral fate, we bind ourselves into some of our most important relationships. Our religion, our spouse, our profession, and sometimes, our country are ours by consent.

Our relationships to all of these include, but cannot be reduced to, a promise or contract. Each one involves a gift that creates the relationship and makes it flourish. That gift cannot be extorted; it can only be offered with consent.

When I take my oath I reveal or express my consent to be bound to stand with others. I do the sort of thing people do when they marry or become naturalized citizens. I use my oath as "words that bind."

After I take my oath I see myself as an officer. In 1890, Justice Brewer wrote, "The taking of the oath of allegiance is the pivotal factor which changes [by which one himself changes] the status from that of civilian to that of soldier." This change need not be the "change of the entire nature of a human creature" that Hume rejected. Still, after I take my oath I regard myself transformed in some way that is not captured by the language of "roles" and "socialization." A former Marine bristles at being called an ex-Marine because he considers himself *to be* a former Marine.

After I take my oath I profess to be an officer. "To profess," according to the *Oxford English Dictionary*, is "to declare openly oneself to be something." Edmund Pellegrio, writing about medical professionalism, has elaborated: "The central act of profession is an active, conscious declaration [revealed vow], voluntarily entered into and signifying willingness [intention] to assume the obligations ["do all manner of things"] necessary to make the declaration authentic." More directly: "This uniform commits us." Every time I present myself in my uniform I profess to be an officer.

Why do I opt to take my oath? The commissioned officer's oath is an oath of acceptance. I opt to accept my commission because I wish to reveal my consent to be bound to others with whom I then stand in a normative relationship as I "discharge the duties of [my] office . . . by doing all manner of things."[8]

AFTERWORD

Those Mental Crossed Fingers. The data collected since 1970 seem to boil down to the result that three out of four young officers are more cavalier about this oath affair—and its impact on officer professionalism—than I suggest. (As I recall, two hundred of us were were ushered in. We raised our right hands, uttered the oath, and departed. So, in fact, my commissioning had little of the import of this philosophical exposition written two decades later.)

If the commissioning oath is potentially as I have proposed, the profession has an opportunity to

introduce, administer, and enforce it as a professional resource. Several institutional implications would
result.

Two Voices. The moral landscape mapped out by the
oath as a revealed vow is different from the terrain
of the oath as the source of promissory obligations,
rights, and demands. The difference is as old as the
contrast between Aristotle's ethics of character and
an ethics of acts. Admiral Stockdale and Colonel
Wakin have urged the military to heed such a distinction; John Ladd and William May have done the
same for the medical professional. A related issue in
current women's studies is the difference between a
morality of rights and formal requirements and a
morality of care and responsibility. A *Great Ideas
Syntopicon* chapter explores the influence that a similar distinction has had on concepts of Duty.

The language of promises is rooted in individu-
als-as-selves; it is impartial, universal, and suited to
strangers. Its negative, minimal, legalistic ground
rules function like "rules of grammar." Transmitted
by pre-existing rules, promise language is backed by
sanctions. Its rights and demands are last-ditch
stands; we go to lawyers when we are in trouble.

The language of revealed vows is rooted in indi-
viduals-as-related; it befits more permanent and personal relations. Maximal and positive, revealed-vow
language concedes the diversity of proximate situations and works like suggestions for "sublime and
elegant style." Shown by example, it exhorts and
challenges with rewards and expresses disdain for
unbefitting conduct. "When men are friends they
have no need of justice." (Aristotle, *NE* 1155a).

Insidious Creeping Legalism. The duty to do "all manner of things" can be "positively strangled" (Stockdale) and involves an aspiration that is "flattened out" (Leon Fuller) by the requirements of promissory obligations.

Gyges' Ring. Without swords, revealed vows are still revealed vows. Socrates put that vow in the soul. Colonel Heinl's *classicus locus*, "Special Trust and Confidence," calls for an institution that nourishes the vow of the individual officer.

Imprecating Heavenly Vengeance. "If I ever break my solemn pledge may I be punished severely by Soviet law, universal hatred and contempt of the working people." The two quotations I used at the beginning of my text point out that, in addition to violating the UCMJ or the Code of Conduct, an officer can somehow also "violate" or "betray" his oath. Officers are no longer cashiered out fast and ignobly, but the *Marine Corps Manual* describes a climate in which "special trust and confidence . . . jeopardized by the slightest transgression [and] any offense . . . will be dealt with promptly, and with sufficient severity." December 1988 news accounts reported that following a tragic event, the Marine Corps planned to court martial a lieutenant and had relieved two other officers of their commands. A fair reading is that all three failed to do "all manner of things," that the lieutenant violated some UCMJ contractual obligations of his oath, and that the other two officers violated the vow of their oath by failing to do some special trust and confidence "things." Historically oaths have been backed by sanctions.

Michael Corleone (The Godfather). He was a Catholic, a member of the Mafia, a husband, and a Marine Corps captain all by "mere will and consent." Every military call for complete loyalty or ultimate commitment betrays provincialism.

Brigadier General Savage (Twelve O'clock High). "It's easy to transfer out of a group; it's pretty hard for a man to transfer out of his obligation [and still harder to transfer out of his vow] but then every man has to play it the way he [with *his vow*] sees it." This statement describes an institution attentive to dissent (of Siegfried Sassoon, for example).[9]

NOTES

Acknowledgment: Captain Richard A. Stratton, USN (Ret.), presented the JSCOPE version of this essay on my behalf. It is a pleasure to thank Dick for his support.

1. In 1988 I challenged the practice of attempting to determine a commissioned officer's sworn obligations by appealing to his oath (U.S. Naval Institute *Proceedings*, December 1988, p. 92). Quotations in this essay are drawn from the references, unless noted.

2. Edward Coffman (*Parameters*, September 1987) presents the American case; see Edgar Denton's *Limits of Loyalty* for the European claim.

3. The conclusion that the text itself has little impact on actual practice explains why a naval captain, an army major general, and a former commandant of the Marine Corps are among those who have mistakenly cited the oath's text in recent public record.

4. The "triangle" is borrowed from Donald Baucom (*Air University Review*, September/October 1983). The (religious)

idea of commitment to a picture—used by Wittgenstein—is presented in chapter 3 of Roger Trigg's *Reason and Commitment*. The "sketch of a dramatic part" is developed by Gerald Postema in David Luban's *The Good Lawyer*.

5. The questions are from Hume's *Treatise*, book III, section V, part II. My answers elaborate the views of Michael Robins (cited in the references).

6. Socially based accounts of promising dominate contemporary philosophy (see Robins). They include appeals to fairness and gratitude and reference to a socially accepted convention simply a keep a promise.

7. The quotation is a paraphrase with emphasis added from Levinson, p. 1452. This passage aside, I am indebted to his thesis that an oath's function can be to bind.

8. Studies of military professionalism continue to overlook the fact that an enlisted Marine's first promotion warrant begins: "reposing special trust and confidence."

9. James Webb in the *Naval War College Review* (Winter 1988) refers to Seigfreid Sassoon's declaration of protest in World War I as "a *moral* aspect of strategy." See also James McClung, "Leadership, Followership, and Dissent," *Marine Corps Gazette*, August 1986.

REFERENCES

Brand, C.E., *Roman Military Law*. Austin: University of Texas Press, 1968.

Heinl, R.D., "Special Trust and Confidence." *Proceedings* May 1956; reprinted *Marine Corps Gazette*, May 1984.

James, D.N., "Promising as a Foundation of Medical Ethics." chapter 5 of *"What is Professional Ethics?"* Ph.D. dissertation, Vanderbilt University, 1981.

Kittay, E.V. and D.T. Meyeis, eds. *Women and Moral Theory*. Rowman and Littlefield, 1987.

Ladd, J., "Legalism and Medical Ethics." In *Contemporary Issues in Biomedical Ethics*. Edited by J. Davis, et al. Humana Press, 1978.

Levinson, S., "Constituting Communities Through Words That Bind: Reflections on Loyalty Oaths." *Michigan Law Review* (June 1986): 1440-1470.

May, W.F., "Code, Covenant, Contract, or Philanthropy." *Hastings Center Reports* 5 (1975): 29-38.

Miller, G.E., "Public Law and the Military Commander: Responsibility and Authority." *Naval War College Review* 24 (October 1971): 21-26.

Peek, K.L., "Fidelity: The Key Quality." TIG Brief. 1981.

Pellegrino, E.D., "Toward a Reconstruction of Medical Morality: The Primacy of the Act of Profession and the Fact of Illness." *The Journal of Medicine and Philosophy* 4 (1979).

Reese, T.H., "An Officer's Oath." *Military Law Review* (July 1964): 1-41.

Robins, M.H., *Promising, Intending and Moral Autonomy*. Cambridge University Press: New York, 1984.

Sliving, H., "The Oath," Part 1 and Part 2. *The Yale Law Review* 68 (June and July): 1329-1390 and 1526-1577.

Stockdale, J.B., "Taking Stock." *Naval War College Review* (Fall 1978).

Winthrop, W., *Military Law and Precedents*. Hein 1979.

(No author cited) "Oath of Allegiance." *Soviet Military Review* 2 (1978).

CAREERISM IN THE MILITARY SERVICES: A MORAL ANALYSIS OF ITS NATURE, TYPES, AND CONTRIBUTING CAUSES

JOSEPH C. FICARROTTA
Captain, U.S. Air Force Academy

Captain Ficarrotta looks at moral lapses often described as ca-reerist and finds all of them to be blameworthy independent of their association with careerism. He considers the fundamental moral obligations of service members, and he shows that service members have no moral duty to advance their careers. He regrets that up-or-out policies emphasize promotion as a meassure of the worth of one's service.

In doing a careful inquiry into careerism, we are immediately faced with the problem of clarifying just what we take careerism to be, and as part of this same problem, deciding just what it is about the careerist that we find morally culpable. While I would not characterize this initial step as an overwhelmingly difficult one, it warrants a certain amount of care, for in our everyday discourse, the concept is more often than not muddled and ambiguous. If we hope to correct this problem for the military services, we must first overcome these conceptual and definitional difficulties. After this, we can explore what might be causes of the problem, and look for ways to correct it.

* * *

Producing examples of careerism, or finding individuals we are willing to disparage with the careerist label, is a woefully simple matter. Still, when pressing for an underlying principle, we encounter difficulty. Two approaches might at first blush seem plausible but are ultimately unsatisfying. In the first approach, still more examples of careerism are produced in hope that, even though a precise definition is not being offered, enough exposure to the sin will sharpen our intuitive grasp of it. Reminiscent of a position once taken in the debate over the nature of pornography, this position has it that, while we might not be able to say exactly what careerism is, we can surely know it when we see it. Unfortunately, our senses of recognition are never quite unanimous in the verdicts they render. Even if they were, we would still be left with the more important work of determining just what essential characteristic the many different examples of careerism had in common. Our list could easily include much bureaucratic "square filling" to enhance one's promotion potential, certain types of maneuvering for better positions, the sychophancy we call "boot licking" (and other less flattering military colloquialisms for the same sort of activity), Machiavellian "back stabbing," or even sending troops to unnecessary death for the sake of good appearances. All of these disparate types of behavior seem to be examples of careerism, and no common or underlying characteristic is immediately obvious.

The second approach goes a little further—and asserts that careerism is the attitude and activity that places one's career above everything else, where everything else is usually couched in terms of responsibilities to others in particular or one's profession in general. While better than the first, this approach still lacks completeness. I want to develop a broader definition that will still account for the notions we have been entertaining but that provides a better conceptual framework for determining what ultimately does and does not count as careerism.

As a starting point, we should notice that ambition is not, of itself, a moral defect. Indeed, a desire to develop professionally and assume as much responsibility as one's talents will permit is usually taken to be normal, healthy, or even virtuous. Long hours and hard work, taking on tough assignments, and a dedication to work that even excludes much free time and recreation might all be viewed as admirable qualities, even if promotion and other rewards are hoped for or expected as an indirect result. Plainly, we can place our careers and the concomitant promotions above a great many things and not commit the moral error that is normally called careerism. In fact, I propose there is only *one* thing that will make us guilty of careerism: the compromising of *some moral principle or principles* in order to advance one's career goals.

While this is certainly not a profound revelation, keeping this in mind helps to bring out some points that might otherwise not be obvious. First, careerism is what I would like to call a derivatively blameworthy activity. We do not find the pursuit of career goals in itself a problem, but instead, it is the immoral means employed in that pursuit that we find distasteful, insofar as those means compromise or totally dispense with some moral principle or princi-ples. Second, seen in this way, it becomes clear that careerism is not a single sin, but a collection of moral transgressions, united only in that they are commit-ted in the same context. Lying, cheating, being disin-genuous in personal relationships, causing needless death or suffering, violating special trusts and the like are all wrong, regardless of *why* they are perpe-trated. It is when a moral transgression is committed in pursuit of career goals that we call it careerism. This being the case, it is always pertinent to ask just what particular moral rule a person has broken that justifies applying the careerist label. Simply refer-ring to the general category of careerism will not do, for once again, this is not a moral defect *per se* but rather a loose collection of more definable defects related in how and where they are displayed.

From what has been said, it should be clear that careerism is closely related to the moral shortcoming of selfishness, and comparing the two might improve our grasp of both. Self-interested motivations, in and of themselves, are not blameworthy. Only when we ignore the interests of others when we *ought not* to are we guilty of selfishness. In fact, if we think of career ambitions as a type of self-interest, we might even view careerism as a subset of selfishness.

Selfishness and careerism also seem amenable to comparison in terms of the moral violations which characterize them. Just as we saw to be the case in careerism, the collection of moral rules, the break-ing of which turns self-interestedness into selfish-ness, is very large and diverse. Lying, neglecting the duty of clarity, ignoring the rights or legitimate dis-tributive justice claims of others, breaking promises, or nearly any other moral transgression will do—if performed in the pursuit of self-interest, it appears to qualify as selfish behavior. The case is likewise for careerism: there are almost as many types of careerism as there are moral rules to be broken (even if, for various reason, some types are more common than others).

*   *   *

I think it will be illustrative to examine some of the various types of careerism. We can begin by pointing to what I will call the "easy" cases of careerism. In these, the activity engaged in is plainly immoral, and could never be morally justified as a means of furthering a career. Moreover, in these easy cases, the moral principle being violated is a simple matter to ascertain.

Needlessly risking (or even spending) the very lives and safety of those under one's command merely for the sake of career progression would be an example of such an easy case. Of course, leading soldiers into battle is not, in and of itself, blameworthy. Nor is it morally suspect for us to promote leaders based in part on their combat experience. The offensive element in this scenario is the fact that lives and safety are disregarded in a cavalier manner, which ought to be renounced in any context. Intentionally causing death and injury, without some powerful, overriding justification, is a grievous offense. Beyond this, in the military environment (as it might be in other environments as well, such as the law enforcement or medical professions), such a disregard for life and safety is exacerbated by the fact that those led invest a special trust in their leaders to take the best care possible of their lives and safety, and that trust is being breached.

A number of other easy cases come to mind, but I will assume that the process of teasing out the particular moral rule being broken would be as simple and obvious as in the case cited above. Blatant lying and cover-up activity, where only one's career is at issue, are another easy case. So are many illegal contracting practices, such as unfairly passing sensitive information to favored bidders, taking bribes and kick-backs, and a host of other related contracting practices; I am sure an expert background in all the subtleties of the government procurement process would be needed to understand and appreciate fully all the ways a person can be a careerist in this way (that is, when these activities go beyond simple thievery and are meant to advance the culprit's military or post-military career). Actively sabotaging another's work or reputation for self-serving motives is another plainly reprehensible undertaking, and would be wrong irrespective of the circumstances.

I hope, perhaps naively, that the particularly nasty collection of easy cases outlined above is not commonplace or representative. The damage done to the military's popular image in past years notwithstanding, I believe the types of activity typical of our easy cases, in that the moral transgressions are blatant, severe, or both, if not rare, are at least relatively uncommon. Unhappily, another group of career advancing practices, characterized by less blatant and less severe violations of moral rules, are all too easily found.

Cultivating disingenuous personal relationships in order to advance one's career is an extremely widespread phenomenon and is such a fixture in professional life that it is often engaged in by the offender without any conscious calculation. General Halftrack's boot-licking Lieutenant Fuzz (from the cartoon strip "Beetle Bailey") is a comical caricature, but the real life manifestations of this type of career-ism are shameless and depressing displays. Often cloaked in or confused with respect for a superior, this practice fails to make the distinction between the military virtue of paying the respect due to a superior's rank or position and ingratiating behavior toward the superior qua individual in hopes of curry-ing favor. It seems incredible that anyone would fall victim to this sort of manipulation, especially when we consider how often we can observe, as disinterest-ed spectators, the boot-licker at work. But the prac-tice is nonetheless all too common, made possible by what I take to be an almost universal feature of human nature: we are vulnerable to flattery, and only the hardest among us are immune.

However widespread this boot-licking phenome-non might be, it is still blameworthy and is careerism when it is employed to advance a career. The rele-vant moral transgression here is using our fellow man for our own ends without consent, through de-ceit, trickery, and manipulation. The con artist or the flimflam man is guilty of the same kind of im-moral conduct toward different ends, as is any other purely self-serving manipulator of others, whatever the context. I also think that in the military environment, violation of the special trust we hope to build between military superiors and subordinates aggravates the severity of this moral shortcoming.

Another extremely widespread practice generally regarded as careerism is often called ticket-punching. A service member knows that certain schools, jobs, assignments, and so forth, more often that not, significantly enhance chances for promotion. Consequently, service members pursue these apparent prerequisites for promotion with single-minded vigor, often to the neglect of primary duties, genuine professional development in a specialty, or the real and pressing needs of the service. The moral rule being violated in this case is less clear. Indeed, one might even argue that it requires some moral courage to resist this form of careerism. After all, the service itself seems to encourage and reward the behavior and in some sense punish those who decline to participate, even if to its own detriment.

What then is the moral transgression of the ticket puncher? I would not go so far as to liken this to taking advantage of a mental defective, but I do find something analogous in not returning an overpayment or not pointing out an oversight in, say, a telephone bill. In contracting for phone service, all the administrative trappings of the billing process are designed to facilitate fair compensation for service rendered. Should something go awry due to one party or another's error, systematic or otherwise, it would seem a duty to point out this deviation from the fair and equitable relationship that was presupposed by both parties. Likewise, any relationship between an employer and an employee makes tacit assumptions of good faith between them, whether it be positive in the form of conscientiousness or negative in the form of prohibitions of dishonesty through omissions.

In the military, much more than a simple contractual relationship is effected (in spite of common sentiments to the contrary), which makes ticket punching that much worse. We take a solemn oath of office which binds us even more firmly in this duty to discharge our responsibilities in good faith. Even if the military wishes its members would behave one way but rewards them when they act differently, it is incumbent upon us with at least some force to recognize "square filling" in the promotion process for the problem it is.

I should point out that not all of what we often call ticket punching is necessarily blameworthy. In an ideal military, the services will outline career development paths, with the concomitant schools, assignments, etc., that actually develop the professional capacity of the officers in ways that make them better able to serve. If this development is then used by the services as criteria for promotion, it would seem that both the service and the potential careerist would be happy with the results.

But even in this ideal situation, I think the primary object of the officer's intentions is critical. If the officer is truly concerned with what I roughly refer to as genuine career development, the officer will not be easily swayed from pursuit of it. On the other hand, if the officer is concerned merely with becoming more competitive for promotion, the individual will pursue whatever he or she believes to be instrumental to that end. Should the service misguidedly start asking for less than helpful career development, the ticket puncher (in the pejorative sense) will immediately abandon previous goals to do whatever is necessary to ensure advancement. Even if the interests of the military and the careerist coincidentally match up by some stroke of luck or master planning, it may not remain intact for any length of time. When the carrot of career progression leads the officer in another direction, there he or she will go. The careerist does not have the interest of the service in the heart but cares only about promotion.

What then ought we to do when faced with this sort of dilemma between genuine career development and promotion? Because this particular transgression is one of the more innocuous in our careerist collection, most will leave resignation, or more slowly but just as surely, the consequences of nonselection for promotion in our 'up or out' system, to the more heroic among us. Regardless, we can still very easily point out the problems inherent in ticket punching or square filling to decision makers as clearly and emphatically as we are able. Additionally, we certainly should do whatever we can short of "abandoning ship" to minimize the impact of these problems on fulfilling what would surely be the enlightened interests of our "employer" in a good faith arrangement.

To our credit, recent reforms in the Air Force have been reasonable practical steps toward controlling this type of careerism. Effort is being made to encourage and reward the actions and career progressions that best serve the needs of the service. If we are successful, the arrangement will approach the ideal we just imagined, and doing the right thing will not require officers to forgo promotion. Of course, changing the character of the potential careerist in ways that would help in less than ideal arrangements would be a more challenging undertaking.

No doubt we could list other types of careerist behaviors and carry out a similar analysis of the relevant moral principles being isolated. Yet even with this short exposition of the various stripes of careerism in mind, I hope the claim I made initially is clearer: to repeat, careerism is not a particular moral defect but rather a collection of transgressions united only in the context in which they occur. Careerist acts are of various types and severities, and we might, in a more detailed investigation, observe more thoroughly how they pan out into categories.

My claim about the pluralistic nature of careerism makes it possible to expose some helpful distinctions that would normally be neglected or remain ambiguous. When we say careerism, do we mean lying? Disingenuous personal relationships? Playing along in an easy way with a defective system? Failing to fulfill the legitimate expectations of others created by our role in society? Or something else? Whenever we use the term, we would do well to be precise about what we mean, for the various types of careerism involve different moral breaches and consequently require different sorts of responses.

* * *

The notion that promotion is a right for every hardworking and competent service member seems to infect the military services at every level. It has fallen below the level of conscious deliberation. Bubbling just below the surface of the military's collective unconscious is the certainty that promotion *is* success. Failure to be promoted *is* failure and failure of the worst kind. It is an ethos that places promotion above all other forms of development and success. Clearly, "be all that you can be" has come to mean in the minds of many "get promoted as high as you can." Following moral rules may or may not be expedient to this end, and the result is too often careerism.

Why has this happened? Are there some identifiable causes of this apparent departure from traditional military values (or explanations as to why this attitude has come to be included in the more traditional set)? Are there any steps we might take to solve this problem or at least avoid aggravating it? I hope fervently that there is something, or some combination of things, that we can do, for this willingness to compromise or dispense with morality in order to enhance promotion opportunities that we call careerism has been, I think, very aptly described as a cancer.

It should be obvious to any member of the military that I have so far neglected a feature of the military promotion system that is extremely important to my project: the consequences, at various points in one's career, of not being promoted. It is with this that I will begin to examine what I believe are at least two of the causes contributing to careerism in the military.

Essentially, failure to get promoted results in loss of one's job. Failure to reach captain or major results in close to immediate dismissal, and failure to reach higher rank shortens the number of years one may remain on active duty before being compelled to retire. These consequences, no doubt, bring a sense of urgency to the promotion process that it would never have without them.

For passed over lieutenants, four or more years of their lives are very nearly wasted, and the stigma of being fired follows them as they leave the service. For the passed over captain, who is forced to start a new career after ten or more years, without the psychological (as well as financial) buffer of a pension, it is a personal disaster indeed. Besides, to make matters worse, the duties one held in the military may or may not provide any basis for civilian employment of comparable quality or compensation.

Failure in promotion to general, colonel, and lieutenant colonel can be just as distressing. Being forced to retire at an age when most civilian counterparts consider themselves in the prime of their careers is extremely frustrating. All the more frustrating is the fact that the officer's age is not the reason for the *de facto* dismissal—obviously those who are promoted seem to get along just fine in spite of their "advanced" age and the presumably more demanding responsibilities presented by the higher rank. Failure at these points costs them years of doing what had become their life's work and forces them to start a new career (or more often, merely a job) at a time when they might be attending to their most important achievements.

Even during the years that nonselectees to the senior ranks are permitted to remain, we see frustration and what amounts to punishment as a result of their nonselection. Only the dead end jobs come one's way; only the less desirable and less challenging assignments are available. The failure to be promoted is a stone around one's neck, even at levels that the service itself ostensively regards as a moderately successful career. Witness the past treatment of passed over lieutenant colonels, and the dichotomous fast-track and pre-retirement possibilities available to colonels.

Obviously, some of the officers we pass over are people we would just as soon see move along anyway. Even so, many perfectly competent and dedicated officers are forced to leave the service not because they are ineffective in their present duties, but rather because they do not show the potential for higher rank. Worse, this potential is often judged based on the questionable criteria embraced by the ticket puncher.

These unhappy retention and retirement policies do create a practical pressure to get promoted, which might derive some moral force from other considerations. More precisely, I think most of us would agree that people do have a duty to take a certain minimal amount of care and responsibility for their own welfare. In this and other situations this translates into a duty to find and hold a job. It is this duty which creates culpability, when there is any, for being unemployed. I am sure this up or out approach as practiced in the military contributes heavily to the formation in many people of deeply ingrained, if for the most part unexamined, feelings that we have a moral duty to get promoted.

What sort of weight might this real or perceived duty to get promoted bring into a situation with the potential for careerism? It could bring claims into a moral conflict as a justification for violating other moral rules or duties in the pursuit of career goals. After all, it is conceivable that someone with a hungry family might justly violate some less pressing moral rules to improve his desperate situation, even if it is less plausible to sanction moral shortcoming to procure luxury. Perhaps the threat of losing a job could bring moral, in addition to practical and psychological, pressures to bear on the potential careerist.

I believe that an officer's obligations to country, service, and fellow would always outweigh whatever duties to self-promotion one might have. Hence, I do not believe that it would be easy, or even possible, to produce an example of what might be called justifiable careerism. Still, I will not argue for this here. More important is the weaker claim that many people *do* take it that their careers are of moral importance, and use them as justification for careerist behavior when they should not. Even if there are some cases of justifiable careerism, most often attempts to justify this sort of behavior look more like rationalization than reason-giving to me. Regardless, it is not necessary that we come to a consensus before moving on. The up or out policy is a primary motivator for much careerist thinking and is, because of this, pernicious.

To be fair, we should note that some egoistic tendencies surely come with the new service member via the Western culture. Insofar as this is true, it is a problem much larger than military leaders alone could ever hope to address. We can do next to nothing about the "hard-core" careerist, who lusts pathologically after promotion to the exclusion of observing moral rules. All we can do in these cases is be vigilant and do our best to avoid rewarding those who choose the immoral path, as we would in any endeavor. No change in the present system would significantly discourage this type of careerist in the formation of his designs.

Even so, the up or out promotion system exacerbates any tendencies one might have to pursue promotion through morally defective means. Were we to modify these policies, aside from not encouraging pre-existing moral defectives in our ranks, we would also stop pressuring the ordinary moral everyman who must pass through promotion points to keep his very job. Putting people in these dilemmas is simply not necessary. There are other ways of providing the same benefits (if there are any) as the present system.

One possible objection to reform would have us believe the fierce competition created by the present system makes for better overall performance. Without it, we would find people who reached a certain rank, failed to move higher, and tended to be mediocre in quality. Yet even if this were the case, the services need not be hesitant to remove officers for poor or declining performance, regardless of present rank or pending promotion. There ought always be effective mechanisms in place to relieve promptly those who fail to maintain appropriate proficiency and motivation in their present duties. It is a mistake to use customary promotion points as a sifter for this sort of failing, rather than a sifter for those who desire and are capable of more responsibility.

Another objection to reform points to the need for a young and vigorous military force, and how up or out policies facilitate this. Of course, assuming a youthful and vigorous force is important, it will necessarily be the case that we consider the age of our officers. It would, however, be fallacious to assert that we cannot implement such a policy independent of promotion (or even that the present promotion system is effectively maintaining a youthful force).

Another commonly cited advantage of the present system aims at providing "reasonable" promotion opportunities for newer members of the services. This position assumes it is clearly undesirable for an officer to rise with some certainty to a relatively low rank (perhaps captain), and then wait much longer for, or never get, another chance at being promoted. Against this unqualified assertion, I must counter that having been promoted from the enlisted ranks, I am completely delighted to have reached my present position, am satisfied to remain in it, and do not take this satisfaction to be an unhealthy lack of ambition. I am sure my attitude is not unique. Along these same lines, there are many pilots and other specialists who would be more than happy to remain in the rank of captain, provided they would be allowed to continue in the corresponding duties.

Even if there are great numbers who find reasonable promotion opportunity very important, in an effort to provide better than even chances of promotion at predetermined phases, we have produced a macabre bit of bureaucratic irony. In order to give opportunity to newcomers, we divest ourselves of those with more tenure, merely because they have more tenure! There must be ways to move talented officers up the ranks in an orderly way without dismissing competent people merely for not moving up.

A complete discussion of whether the usual defenses of the up or out system are well founded would properly be the topic of another paper. The important point of my present focus concerns the moral and practical dilemmas it forces on almost every member of the officer corps and the collective effect it is having on us insofar as it encourages careerism. Reform of this system is at least plausible and is most certainly desirable. Enlisted promotion systems in all the services, the specialist program in the U.S. Army, and some features of the Soviet personnel system could all serve as starting points for a serious study of reform.

Another curious notion that I am sure has had some contribution to careerist behavior is the idea that the services somehow *owe* their people promotion opportunities and predictable career (that is promotion) paths in return for a job well done. While this is related to the up or out problem, it is distinct from it in that it is more encompassing. The officer knows how important promotion is and operates under the assumption that meeting certain milestones guarantees at least a reasonable promotion opportunity. In fact, this general idea is typically articulated in subtle (and not so subtle) ways by the institution itself.

As an example of this, we may consider the career (once again, in the minds of many, a poorly disguised euphemism for promotion) planning encouraged by the personnel systems of each service. We can even find official publications that spell out what might be taken as detailed ticket punching plans! Promotion opportunities are promised with what passes for mathematical precision in many a recruiting, retention, and motivational briefing and pamphlet. The opportunity for advancement, if not the centerpiece of each service's employee relation plan, certainly enjoys a prominent place.

This ethos, created in large part by the services themselves, focuses unduly on promotion and brings attention to the process it would not receive otherwise. Indeed, this attention approaches a mania, and the intense emphasis cannot help but contribute to careerist tendencies by blowing the importance of promotion out of proportion.

Yet the conventional wisdom regarding the promotion process is a function of fundamental misunderstandings of the system and its purposes. In point of fact, the needs of the services are (or ought to be) the engine that drives the promotion system; this has always been the truth of the matter. By misleading (more than likely, unintentionally) the officer corps into believing that promotion is intrinsically valuable or some sort of entitlement contingent on a job well done, we have created a myth. If the myth has contributed to careerist attitudes, it has done far more harm than any possible good in the form of morale or motivation.

Given the expectations these widespread attitudes encourage, it should come as no surprise that when better promotion opportunities turn out to be tied to certain specialties, resentment is often the result in those corners with less favorable advancement rates. Of course, when we hold in mind the real purpose of the promotion system, we can see why some specialties enjoy higher promotion rates then others. That is because certain specialities provide a better background for what we need in our senior leaders.

Failure to hold one of these specialties (and hence to be privy to the more favorable promotion opportunities) should not be taken as a mark of inadequacy or limitation. More, I would think that we *cannot* allow this wrong-headed view to take hold or remain in place—a military needs motivated and talented officers in every specialty. But a measure of success and accomplishment for the military that is concerned primarily with promotion encourages these attitudes. Aggravating any attempts to overcome this misconception are the widespread ideas that promotion is everything and owed to everyone for a job well done, and the up or out system that punishes those who fail in the process. As we might expect, the careerist scurries blindly for the "blessed" career fields without any regard for his interests, talents, or the needs of the service.

Rectifying this problem will be more challenging than reforming the up or out system. It is not a single policy amenable to scrutiny and reform but a widespread attitude, a nebulous collection of actions by the services that put an unhealthy emphasis on the importance of being promoted. The difficulty of this notwithstanding, we should do whatever we can to remove institutionally encouraged attitudes that see promotion as the ultimate end of any career, and the sole measure of a service member's contribution to the mission.

* * *

To summarize, I believe careerism involves compromising some moral rule or rules in the pursuit of career advancement, and it is this compromise in and of itself that we find blameworthy, not the career-pursuing context in which it occurs. In this view, it is clear that careerism is not a single sin but a collection of moral shortcomings tied together only by this common context. There are almost as many different types of careerism as there are moral rules to be broken. Further, these various types of careerism carry with them varying degrees of culpability, from barely blameworthy to heinous.

I also pointed out what I see as two major causes of careerism, the up or out promotion system and the willingness of the services to portray the purposes and importance of promotion in ways that are unhealthy and counterproductive. I recommend reforming our promotion and retention policies and rethinking our methods of motivating the officer corps in ways that put much less emphasis on promotion. The damage careerism is doing to the very fabric of our officer corps far outweighs any advantages we might be realizing under the status quo in these matters.

While I have made a few observations concerning the contributing causes of careerism and some possible corrective actions, I have obviously chosen to defer detailed discussion of these and some other germane issues. Still, I hope what I have presented about what careerism *is* at bottom will help in the pressing practical matter of combatting it.

꧁ ꧂

SOLDIERS, UNJUST WARS, AND TREASON

A. DWIGHT RAYMOND
Captain, U.S. Army

Captain Raymond discusses Operation Valkyrie, the attempted assassination of Hitler by senior German officers. Raymond uses the ethical dilemmas faced by these officers to identify the limits beyond which obedience and loyalty cease to be virtues.

It is widely accepted that *jus in bello* principles cannot be overridden because of military necessity.[1] The responsibility of soldiers in this regard is clear; they may not adopt measures that harm innocents or that are excessively cruel. These proscriptions are recognized by law, and a soldier's obedience is required to legal orders only; indeed, he has the duty to disobey illegal ones.

Although a debate will probably always exist as to the precise limits of noncombatant immunity and excessive cruelty, an assumption that the virtues of obedience and loyalty can almost never permit the violation of *jus in bello* principles poses a terrible dilemma. Does the soldier fighting for an unjust cause have the obligation to perform his duty regardless, or does he have a duty or right to follow higher values?

The dilemma is perhaps best demonstrated by the German High Command during World War II. Some members were involved in Operation Valkyrie, the plot to assassinate Hitler, while others, such as

Guderian, von Manstein, and Keitel, fought effectively as long as they were able. Many in both groups displayed revulsion with the actions of those in the other. General Adolf Heusinger, one of the conspirators, summarized their dilemma:

> Let us not forget what such a decision entails for a soldier—
> an officer raises his hand, at the height of the conflict,
> against his supreme commander . . . even though he is con-
> vinced that his murderous act can on no account prevent his
> country's unconditional surrender to the enemy. He still
> goes through with it, in the hope of sparing his people from
> even greater suffering. . . . [The] people themselves will
> condemn him because they still believe in the Fuhrer. . . .
> Most of the soldiers at the front believe that their only
> salvation lies in a concerted resistance to the external ene-
> my. For them Hitler is still the symbol of the struggle and
> their talisman of victory.

This officer is flying in the face of all the principles of military discipline. How then is he to secure the obedience of his subordinates? He is destroying loyalty, so who will remain loyal to him? In the eyes of many of his comrades he is committing an assault on honor itself. . . . He has reminded his men a hundred times of the sacred nature of their undertaking to do their duty. Two million German soldiers have gone to their death to uphold it. . . . The oath of allegiance is more than a matter of form—he has sworn before God.

One might reply, But would God require him to respect such an oath? This then is the soldier's crisis of conscience. Everyone had to fight this battle in his own heart. There could be no resolution on principle that would be valid for everyone, only tragic and unresolvable contradictions between two different conceptions of duty. If he were faithful to one of them, he would be derelict in the other. Who was wrong? Such things are not for mere men to decide.[2]

Which actions were correct, or are the decisions matters of individual judgment? Whatever the answer, the implications are likely to be problematic.

If the conspirators were right, then at some point a soldier has the right, perhaps even the obligation, to overthrow his political leadership if that leadership's ends are seen to be unjust, implying that military discipline and civilian rule are subordinate to other principles. If Operation Valkyrie was legitimate, a Pandora's Box is opened. Perhaps, the lid would only be cracked open a bit in extreme circumstances, but even so, we have the problem of identifying the precise conditions for opening the box, as for example, when many in the American military opposed the involvement in Vietnam. Would they have been justified in overthrowing the government for prosecuting an unjust war?[3]

If those not involved in Operation Valkyrie were correct in adhering to the principle of duty, other problems arise. Some might argue that if one is required to obey just orders in an unjust war, then this weakens the requirement to disobey unjust orders in a just war. This is because the virtue of obedience is elevated and that of justice is diminished in the soldier's calculation.

If obedience is paramount, the soldier is reduced to the status of an automaton. He is nothing more than a powerful tool that can be used to achieve whatever ends a political leadership decides. He forfeits his right to act as a free moral agent. We might wonder if this denial of the soldier's right of conscience in any way threatens similar rights of other citizens who also have some perceived duty to the state. This danger may be more real in societies that have a large reserve manpower pool; however, it may also appear in any modern society where the distinction between combatant and noncombatant is blurred.

In these two contending views, either (1) there is an objective way of knowing when an Operation Valkyrie would be proper or (2) an Operation Valkyrie can never be proper. If we reject both of these outlooks, we seem to be left with the proposition that individuals must determine for themselves when justice demands action and what action to take. This is certainly not a clean solution and may not be very illuminating. We might conclude that both the Valkyrie conspirators and the loyal officers acted properly; this does not provide soldiers any valuable guidance for the future. Moreover, this view would appear to tolerate civil wars and power struggles, without a clear means of determining which side is right. As long as the combatants are true believers, they all can be viewed as acting correctly.

Cogent arguments to support any of the views can be presented. Believing that there can be no moral division of labor, Robert Nozick categorically states that "it is a soldier's responsibility to determine if his side's cause is just; if he finds the issue tangled, unclear, or confusing, he may not shift the responsibility to his leaders."[4] This flat statement presumes that the justness of a war is to some degree self-evident; however, in reality it is often not very clear. Many still contend that the Vietnam war, if not very smart from the American standpoint, was nevertheless fought for legitimate reasons. Even the charge of unjust German aggression during World War II is contested by some who argue that it was launched in mortal necessity . . . the only serious attempt to destroy the Communist enemy of Western liberties and conscience. [The Nazis] left to defend two thousand years of the highest civilization . . . The Soviets defeating the Reich—that would be Stalin mounting the body of a Europe which, its powers of resistance exhausted, was ready to be raped. . . . People will regret the defeat in 1945 of the defenders and builders of Europe.[5]

We may see these opinions as nothing more than confused propaganda; nevertheless, we must concede that these views, however mistaken, were actually held by some of the Nazi participants.

Michael Walzer states that soldiers do not have the *responsibility* to wrestle with the larger question *jus ad bellum*.[6] This frees the soldier, and it frees us from judging him on these grounds. We might then ask if the soldier has the *right* to consider *jus ad bellum*, and, if so, how may he act? In blunt terms, what we are asking is, When, if ever, is the soldier permitted to commit treason?

To answer questions about treason and soldiers, we must consider the soldier's role, foundations for obedience, how loyalty is articulated and obtained, and the limits of loyalty. The soldier exists to defend his nation-state and, by extension, its interests. He can be called upon to risk his life; the soldier's life, in effect, becomes subordinate to a higher cause.[7] We might speculate that if a soldier's life is an expendable commodity, then his conscience must be expendable as well, as it is merely a subcomponent of that life. This, however, will be rejected out-of-hand; some people choose to fight and die for matters of conscience. Additionally, as hazardous as the soldier's activities are, they are rarely of an absolutely suicidal nature; a soldier still hopes to preserve his life and, presumably, his conscience. It is widely accepted that soldiers are implementors, not makers, of policy; this view was held by the German High Command as strongly as it is held by the American military today.[8] Discipline and loyalty are required both to create a functioning military and to ensure that the military is used in the interests of the society it defends. It is normally seen as virtuous for a soldier to follow orders he dislikes or disagrees with.[9]

Obedience has a moral grounding in addition to its functional one. John Rawls writes that "if the basic structure of a society is just, or as just as it is reasonable to expect in the circumstances, everyone has a natural duty to do what is expected of him."[10] Certainly, we expect the military to follow its orders and to fight required wars. At first glance, we do not expect soldiers to second-guess and resist their directives from legitimate political authority. Edgar Denton III writes that as citizens "we obey the laws of the state, not because the laws are always right, but because we consider it right to obey the law."[11] He further notes that, according to Socrates,

> in any conflict between the state and god [and by god he meant perfect good, perfect justice] god must take priority; in any conflict between man [and by man he meant human self-interest] and the state, the state should prevail. . . . The state must be dissuaded but not disobeyed.[12]

In general, the state attempts to enact positive laws in accordance with natural laws. Citizens (and soldiers) are usually obliged to follow positive laws, even when they conflict with the individual's interpretation of natural laws. Rawls cites a general duty to comply even with unjust laws, noting that "the injustice of a law is not, in general, a sufficient reason for not adhering to it."[13] Rawls does not address "treason" per se, but notes that civil disobedience cannot be "grounded solely on group or self-interest. Instead, one invokes the commonly shared conception of justice that underlies the political order."[14] Such disobedience, furthermore, must be a public act, conducted "openly with fair notice, not covert or secretive."[15]

A soldier's loyalty is not without tensions. West Point's motto "Duty, Honor, Country," is often expanded to the military in general as an appropriate ethical standard, and all three facets can compete with each other under certain circumstances. We might wonder which facet trumps which, and it is often unclear which has been operative. The Iran-Contra arms issues can be cast in several ways vis-a-vis the role of Lieutenant Colonel Oliver North. He may have been dutiful in his obedience to the directives or hints of his superiors,[16] while letting his personal integrity and the good of the nation take a back seat. Alternatively, he may have felt a moral imperative to assist the Contras that he believed overrode his duty to adhere to legalities. Finally, he may have felt that the nation's interest dominated all other considerations.

Thus, any of the three facets of the code could have been tapped to justify North's particular course of action. In many situations, however, the three will compel differing actions. Those participants in Operation Valkyrie appear to have stressed "Country,"[17] while those who remained obedient emphasized "Duty." An officer who valued "Honor" above all, presumably, would have resigned during the early years of the war, when such practice was allowed. In the later years, he probably would have willingly accepted a court-martial and possibly worse.

A soldier's loyalty is often codified in an oath. A priori, the oath should delineate actions required of and prohibited an officer and should indicate the foundation to which a soldier's loyalty is ultimately tied. The oath for U.S. Army officers follows:

> I, (NAME) having been appointed an officer in the Army of the United States, as indicated above in the grade of (RANK) do solemnly swear (or affirm) that I will support and defend the Constitution of the United States against all enemies, foreign and domestic, that I will bear true faith and allegiance to the same, that I take this obligation freely, without any mental reservation or purpose of evasion; and that I will well and faithfully discharge the duties of the office upon which I am about to enter; SO HELP ME GOD.

The oath for German soldiers during World War II was somewhat more terse:

> Before God I swear absolute obedience to the Fuhrer of the Reich and of the German people, Adolf Hitler, supreme commander of the Wehrmacht. As a brave soldier I will be prepared at all times to lay down my life for this oath.

Both oaths seem to lock in the soldier, and seem to resolve potential moral conflicts between state laws and higher laws. The American oath may permit a conflict between "the duties of the office" (if this is interpreted to mean obedience to orders) and "domestic enemies" (if one sees the actions of a political leadership as unconstitutional). Nevertheless, if the oaths are accepted as absolutely binding, they seem to provide little maneuver room for the soldier. Thus, the implication is that the Valkyrie participants were wrong, and that the loyal German officers were right. Furthermore, the dutiful nature of the loyal officers had a moral dimension as well.

The Valkyrie participants can be vindicated only if the moral grip of their oaths is loosened. Utilitarian reasoning would do this easily enough, but it would be useful to see if their "treason" had a stronger moral justification. Two issues regarding the German oath can be addressed. First, the Nazi oath of allegiance was to Adolf Hitler, the national leader, and not to Adolf Hitler, the private individual. Hitler, in his role as national leader, had certain responsibilities: to defend the country, to further its interests (arguably), and to preserve its physical and moral well-being. As Philip Flammer notes, when properly framed, loyalty entails a reciprocal relationship. A superior deserves loyalty, but at the same time he is trusted to fulfill the responsibilities of his office.[18] The relationship between trust and loyalty is similar to that between rights and duties. A citizen has duties because his country gives him rights; if a country unjustly denies a citizen his rights, how can he have duties to that country? A strong argument, I believe, can be made that an official whose actions betray the trust of his people cannot legitimately command their loyalty. The fact that Hitler came to power legally was often cited as further argument that loyalty was required. By creating a dictatorship, however, he attempted to deny Germany any peaceful, "legal" means of binding him to the national trust. By betraying that trust he made the flip-side, loyalty, a meaningless concept. The oath, in other words, is a function not only of its words but also of the context of certain presuppositions and tacit understandings. It was natural for the Valkyrie participants to see treason as the only means of restoring trustworthiness to the national leadership. What other choice did they have?

An issue regarding the oath is raised by General Heusinger: Would God require the soldier to respect such an oath? This question may be more than utilitarianism in disguise. The oath attempts to link obedience to some form of divinity. Even if we grant this linkage, could not other values also be linked to divinity and might not these take precedence over an oath to a government or to a political leader?

Rawls writes that government institutions, such as a nation's constitution and the branches of its government, reflect interpretations of just principles. The institutions may have political legitimacy; their moral legitimacy is a separate issue. Even the political legitimacy is not absolute, as the "final court of appeal is not the court nor the executive nor the legislature but the electorate as a whole."[19] The leader derives his legitimacy from his institutional office, and the institution derives its political legitimacy from the will of the people.

Popular opinion, then, may provide guidance as to which acts may be politically legitimate. It does not, however necessarily tap any degree of moral legitimacy. To appeal to popular opinion would at times be a morally incomplete practice; the masses may sometimes be wrong. (Guderian wrote that in 1944 "the great proportion of German people still believed in Hitler.")[20] Also, it is not always possible to obtain a referendum when seeking moral guidance. Nevertheless, it would seem that a just popular belief should override the clearly unjust desires of a leader; this is strengthened if we affirm that a leader's legitimacy is ultimately traced to the people.

Rawls offers additional advice that is more germane. He notes that the "natural duty not to be made the agent of a grave misjustice outweighs [one's] duty to obey."[21] This implies that even though one's oath may be grounded in a divine foundation, the broader concept of justice is grounded even more firmly.

We can discern some possible limits to the loyalty that is required of soldiers. Denton's consideration of the issue is particularly well-reasoned. Especially for a soldier, the benefit of the doubt must go to the state and to the law. In extreme cases, however, disobedience may be legitimized; this disobedience "should be limited to what is unquestionably an injustice which, if rectified, should establish a basis for a return to obedience."[22] Nazi Germany was one such extreme case. A more recent example was the Philippines military involvement in the ouster of President Marcos. Subsequent factional intrigues against President Aquino, however, would not have met the criterion nor would a hypothetical American military revolt during the Vietnam war. In neither case was it clear that an unjust political institution merited betrayal by the military nor would the military have imposed a more just cure. Coups in third world countries that replace a dictator with a democratic government would be legitimate; however, it should be noted that most past cases have merely resulted in another dictator.

The soldier may indeed presume that a war his nation enters into is just and should follow all just orders in a just manner. He cannot, however, be prohibited from reflecting on the nature of the war and developing his own independent judgment. Again, from Rawls, "in a democratic society . . . each citizen is responsible for his interpretation of the principles of justice and for his conduct in the light of them."[23] If the war is indeed repugnant to the soldier's sense of justice, he is first obliged to resign,[24] whereupon we might expect him to pursue "public acts of civil disobedience." In societies where resignation is not an option (such as the Third Reich during the last years of the war) and the threat to justice is extremely grave, treason such as that committed by the Valkyrie participants is morally permissible.[25]

Several points must be made. First, the soldier may make this determination, but he is not required to.[26] It is impractical to contend that different individuals will reach identical judgments, particularly regarding a topic that is inherently contrary to the individuals' profession. In other words a soldier should not be faulted for remaining loyal, even when popular sentiment, some of his comrades, or history would argue that he should have committed treason. Liddell Hart's observation, while overstated, captures an important aspect: "The German generals of this war were the best-finished product of their profession—anywhere. They could have been better if their outlook had been wider and their understanding deeper. But if they had become philosophers they would have ceased to be solders."[27] Officers like Guderian, von Manstein, and von Rundstedt can justifiably be seen as dedicated professionals worthy of emulation. It is the primary responsibility of the political leadership to ensure that the professional competence of its military is not abused.

A second point to note, justified treason is an exceptional act for exceptional circumstances. The precise conditions are subject to debate, and whether the conditions have been met at a given time is subject to interpretation. The line-drawing problem is not unique to this issue, and we should perhaps recall that "the fact of twilight does not mean you cannot tell day from night."[28]

Another point should be noted; in Denton's words,

> The validity of resistance to and disobedience of the commands of the state depends, in the final analysis, upon the motivation behind that resistance and disobedience. If the motivation is irrational egoism, eccentricity, or self-interest, social, political, or economic, then disobedience is fundamentally immoral.[29]

In other words, treason motivated by concerns for justice is sometimes permissible in order to prevent a great evil. If, however, von Stauffenberg had attempted to assassinate Hitler after receiving a payment from the Russians, the act would have been flatly wrong. Naturally, different motives can exist; this entangles the problem and makes moral judgments even more difficult. It is worth noting that "revisionist" portrayals of Operation Valkyrie contend that the participants were not concerned about justice at all; rather, they turned on Hitler merely because the war had taken a turn for the worse.

Finally, the inherent risk of treason must be stressed. Heusinger's account reflects this quite well, and Denton states that the individual must and will act in the way his moral principles demand. . . . [H]e will take the responsibility for his actions, knowing full well that only the thin line of fate separates the hero from the villain and the patriot from the rebel.[30]

These conclusions should be acceptable whether one ultimately grounds his beliefs in human rights or justice. Certainly, the soldier retains some right of conscience; this right would be violated if in patently extreme cases he was forced to be an evil agent. Additionally, a concern for universal human rights, if these rights are absolute, would compel disobedience to a regime that was a gross violator. Conversely, it would seem that a soldier has the right to concentrate on the mechanics of his duties and to be free from a moral guessing game as to whether his political leadership is acting justly. Moreover, the citizens of a country have a basic right of physical security; inherent in this right is a confidence that the military will be reliable. This right is not enhanced by a military that makes its own fragmented judgments about what it should or should not do.

Justice in the Aristotelian tradition requires that an individual both provide and receive that which his role requires. It would, seemingly, be unfair to vilify a soldier for being loyal in fulfillment of his role. From a liberal Rawlsian view, however, the paramount issue is the just nature of institutions. An unjust institution legitimizes actions taken against it, if these actions result in a just replacement.

In holding that loyalty is *almost* always allowed and that treason is *sometimes* permitted, we are left with at least two disturbing conclusions. First, some moral decisions are within the realm of subjective individual evaluation, even in the disciplined, regimented life of the soldier. There are reasons that would justify treason. We do not, however, have a clear-cut template that can easily be applied to all cases. What is more, such a formula may not even be desirable; it would be subject to grave abuse; it would intensify the ethical dilemma of the soldier to the point of paralysis; and it would necessitate post-treason condemnation of and recriminations against loyal soldiers who may have acted in good faith.

Secondly, there are limits to what a society can expect of its military. A society may not be able to disregard morality in its policies and then expect the military to follow its bidding. I have argued that under certain conditions a soldier may be permitted to object. It is only a short additional step to a position that states a soldier should, in fact, do so.

NOTES

1. One might conceive of very extreme situations where a moral agent might want to bend *jus in bello* principles. One might argue on utilitarian grounds that a catastrophe should be prevented if the cost is quite small.

2. Pierre Galante, *Operation Valkyrie: The German Generals' Plot against Hitler* (New York: Harper & Row, 1981), p. 246.

3. See page 66.

4. Robert Nozick, *Anarchy, State, and Utopia* (New York: Basic Books, 1974), p. 100.

5. Leon Degrelle, *Campaign in Russia: The Waffen SS on the Eastern Front* (Torrance, Ca: 1985), pp. xi, 4, 10, 11.

6. Michael Walzer, *Just and Unjust Wars* (New York: Basic Books, 1977), p. 304.

7. Ibid., chap. 9.

8. See "In Retrospect" in F.W. von Mellenthin, *Panzer Battles* (New York: Ballantine Books, 1956). Also Walzer, p. 289: "aggression is first of all the work of political leaders."

9. A classic example of this is the case of General Edwin Walker, who commanded the 101st Airborne Division when it was tasked to enforce desegregation laws in Little Rock, Arkansas, in 1957. He performed his duties flawlessly, despite the fact that he was an extreme conservative who vehemently opposed desegregation. William Manchester, *The Glory and the Dream* (Boston: Little, Brown and Co., 1973), p. 986.

10. John Rawls, *A Theory of Justice* (Cambridge: Harvard University Press, 1971), p. 334. Note that this leaves some room for subjective interpretation. What is "reasonably just under the circumstances?" A government that is 99 percent just? 50 percent? 10 percent?

11. Edgar Denton III, *Limits of Loyalty* (Waterloo, Canada: Wilfrid Laurier University Press, 1980), p. 11.

12. Ibid., pp. 12-13.

13. Rawls, *A Theory of Justice*, p. 350.

14. Ibid., p. 365.

15. Ibid., p. 366.

16. Particularly in the military, fine lines exist between orders, suggestions, and hints; they all normally elicit the same responses.

17. German law differentiates between treason against the government (hochverrat) and treason against the country (landesverrat); Denton, p. 102.

18. Malham M. Wakin, ed., *War, Morality, and the Military Profession* (Boulder: Westview Press, 1986), chap. 11.

19. Rawls, *A Theory of Justice*, p. 390.

20. Heinz Guderian, *Panzer Leader* (London: Futura Publications, 1952), p. 349.

21. Rawls, *A Theory of Justice*, p. 380.

22. Denton, *Limits of Loyalty*, p. 19.

23. Rawls, *A Theory of Justice*, p. 390.

24. Walzer, *Just and Unjust Wars*, p. 294. However, von Manstein, in *Lost Victories*, stated that resignation by members of the High Command would have been unfair to front-line troops who did not have the luxury of walking away from the war.

25. I have not addressed the morality of assassination; it is certainly not taken for granted that it is a permissible action, even if treason can be condoned. Guderian writes of the July 20th attempt: "For myself I refuse to accept murder in any form. Our Christian religion forbids it in the clearest possible terms. I cannot therefore approve of the plan of assassination" (p. 348.) The act was also of debatable morality when one considers that the bomb was indiscriminate, killing and injuring other persons who may have been innocent. Indeed, one of the injured persons was General Heusinger, a member of the Valkyrie conspiracy.

26. Some argue that high-ranking officers are less able to claim obedience as a justification for their actions. Such was the rationale for the executions of Keitel and Jodl after World War II. If this is indeed the case, judgments concerning the levels at which soldiers acquire additional responsibility must be made. I would contend that if the Joint Chiefs of Staff are accountable political leaders, they are no more so than Cabinet members and congressmen.

27. B. H. Liddell Hart, *The German Generals Talk* (New York: Quill, 1948), p. 300.

28. Quoted in Richard A. Wasserstrom, *War and Morality* (Belmont, CA: Wadsworth Publishing Company, 1970), p. 52.

29. Denton, p. 19.

30. Denton, p. 19.

BIBLIOGRAPHY

Cohen, Marshall; Nagel Thomas; and Scanlon Thomas, eds. *War and Moral Responsibility*. Princeton: Princeton University Press. 1974.

Croker, Lawrence P. *The Army Officer's Guide* (42nd ed). Harrisburg, PA: Stackpole Books, 1983.

Denton, Edgar, III. *Limits of Loyalty*. Waterloo, Canada: Wilfrid Laurier University Press, 1980.

Department of the Army. *The Bedrock of Our Profession*. Washington, DC: U.S. Government Printing Office, 1986.

Dyer, Gwynne. *War*, New York: Crown Publishers, 1985.

Gorlitz, Walter, ed. *The Memoirs of Field-Marshal Keitel*. New York: Stein and Day, 1966.

A. DWIGHT RAYMOND

Guderian, Heinz. *Panzer Leader*. London: Futura Publications, 1952.

Keegan, John, and Richard Holmes. *Soldiers*. New York: Elisabeth Sifton Books, 1986.

Liddell Hart, B. H. *The German Generals Talk*. New York: Quill Books, 1948.

Liddell Hart, B.H. *The Rommel Papers*. New York: Harcourt, Brace and Company, 1953.

Macksey, Kenneth. *Guderian: Creator of the Blitzkrieg*. New York: Stein and Day, 1975.

Manchester, William. *The Glory and the Dream*. Boston: Little, Brown, and Co., 1973.

Paskins, Barrie and Michael Dockrill. *The Ethics of War*. Minneapolis: University of Minnesota Press, 1979.

Rawls, John. *A Theory of Justice*. Cambridge: Harvard University Press, 1971.

Shirer, William L. *The Rise and Fall of the Third Reich*. New York: Fawcett Crest, 1959.

Speer, Albert. *Inside the Third Reich*. New York: The MacMillan Company, 1970.

Wakin, Malham M., ed. *War, Morality, and the Military Profession*. Boulder: Westview Press, 1986.

Walzer, Michael. *Just and Unjust Wars*. New York: Basic Books, 1977.

Wasserstrom, Richard A. *War and Morality*. Belmont, CA: Wadsworth Publishing Company, 1970.

Wenker, Kenneth H. *Foundations of Professional Morality*. Colorado Springs: United States Air Force Academy, 1985.

PART II

PROFESSIONS WITHIN
A PROFESSION

≈⟋⟍≈

COMMANDERS, STAFF JUDGE ADVOCATES, AND THE ARMY CLIENT

DENNIS F. COUPE
Colonel, U.S. Army

Colonel Coupe discusses rules published in 1987 to clarify the ethical requirements of Army lawyers, whose client is the Department of the Army but who work directly for individual commanders. Like other service members, Army lawyers are autonomous moral agents who must be prepared to deal responsibly with conflicting loyalties.

On June 3, 1987, after two years of staffing by Army and joint service legal representatives, the Army judge advocate general approved a policies and procedures document, the *Rules of Professional Conduct for Lawyers*.[1] The new ethical rules were published as a Department of the Army pamphlet and subsequently incorporated in the Army regulation on military justice.[2] These rules are the first set of consolidated ethical requirements, guidelines, and commentary drafted specifically for Army lawyers and for civilian lawyers who appear in Army legal proceedings.[3]

Since the origins of the Judge Advocate General's Corps in the Continental Army of 1775, military and civilian lawyers appearing in military proceedings followed the ethical rules of the civilian bar. Uniformed lawyers were bound by the ethical standards of their respective states, regardless of the mil-

itary nature of the proceedings. The absence of
formal ethical standards for practice before courts-
martial or other military legal proceedings was probably attributable to the hybrid, lay-professional nature of lower levels of courts-martial prior to
enactment of the Uniform Code of Military Justice
in 1950.[4] Non-lawyer counsel continued to appear in
lower levels of courts-martial until 1969.[5]

In the past twenty years, military legal proceedings have grown increasingly complex, both proce-
durally and substantively. The practice of military
law expanded from the major areas of military justice, international law, administrative law, claims
contracts, and legal assistance to a multitude of specialized requirements, including labor relations, environmental law, copyright and patent law, tort
litigation, and information law. These new military
needs for legal skills and representation widened the
scope of legal advice from staff judge advocates to
the military commanders. As a result, commanders
and their lawyers are seeing more of each other today than in the past. Command decisions are more
likely than ever before to involve legal issues, either
directly or indirectly. The broader range of the staff
judge advocate-command relationship underscores
the need for clear ground rules, in order to ensure
that no misunderstandings exist as to the limits of
the relationship.

One of the new military justice ethical rules,
rule 1.13, "Army as Client," identifies the Army as
the primary client of command lawyers and staff
judge advocates. Client loyalties and duties to protect confidential communications of the client are
extended first and foremost to the Army, and only

derivatively to commanders and other authorized representatives of the Army. Rule 1.13 clarifies a basic but sometimes not fully understood principle that must govern professional relationships among commanders, command lawyers, and their mutual employer, the U.S. Army: duties of public office—to the Constitution, to the rule of law, and to the government—must prevail if conflicting personal interests arise.

DRAFTER'S INTENT

Before the new Army military justice rules were issued in 1987, published ethical guidance for military and civilian lawyers in Army legal proceedings was limited to the ethical rules applying to all lawyers upon bar admission by their state or federal licensing authorities[6] and to various laws, regulations, Executive orders, and opinions addressing ethically related behavior in particular types of legal or illegal activity.[7]

Service-unique laws, Executive orders, regulations, and procedures can create correspondingly unique ethical situations.[8] Because the ethical rules that the American Bar Association, the states, and even the Federal Bar Association developed generally do not distinguish between civilian and military practice, a need existed for a consolidated set of rules, guidelines, and examples of ethical conduct tailored to the specialized military setting. The Army *Rules of Professional Conduct for Lawyers* publication is intended to meet this need.

The Army describes the lawyer as "a representative of clients, an officer of the legal system, and a public citizen having special responsibility" for the improvement of justice by virtue of a license to practice law.[9] The responsibilities to clients, to the courts, to the law, and to the improvement of justice are "usually harmonious."[10] As commissioned military officers, uniformed lawyers have additional obligations to their oaths of office and to their military supervisors. This role of the officer is compatible with a lawyer's role, except in the rare circumstance where a conflict occurs between what the military obligations require and what a lawyer may do. Army guidance provides the dovetailing of professional obligations of uniformed legal officers, both as lawyers obligated to the ethical standards of their licensing jurisdictions and as military officers obligated to obey the law.

Lawyers who practice in military proceedings, especially military lawyers who represent the U.S. Government, can encounter ethical situations unknown to private practitioners. Probably the most common examples arise from the multifaceted responsibilities of commanders of both major units and activities, such as commanders of both divisions and installations. Commanders at these and higher senior levels act as quasijudicial officials for military justice purposes and as decisionmaking Army representatives for a variety of administrative actions with legal consequences, in addition to being concerned with their traditional priority: preparation for combat success through necessarily authoritarian means. Identifying the commander's role becomes critical to both the command legal advisor and to the com-

mander to avoid such problems as inadvertent unlawful command influence in military justice
matters.

Should commanders be considered as legal clients of staff judge advocates in the traditional sense,
the same as any lawyer's client and to the same extent as the Army client? More specifically, should the
duties and loyalties that a lawyer owes clients and
should the rational concepts of privileges and confidences be the same for the commander as for the
Army and the U.S. Government, when the client is
the commander and the lawyer is the command legal
advisor, both of whom are subject to their oaths to
support the Constitution? Relatedly, what are the
duties of staff judge advocates and other command
lawyers if conflict occurs between the personal interests of commanders and the interests of the Army
and the U.S. Government?

Military justice ethics, especially rule 1.13, and
the answers to these questions for command lawyers
come from the broader ethical environment, that of
professional military officership. The official Army
position taken is that the ethical obligations of military lawyers in advising their commanders are logical and necessary extensions of the same ethical
obligations that apply to all military officers.

REFLECTING "THE MILITARY ETHIC"

Ethical issues are at the core of the human condition,
confronting us in our lesser or greater roles, whether we are princes or paupers, preachers or politicians, citizens or soldiers.[11] Military service involves

unique ethical as well as legal concerns. As an institution, the military services place great emphasis on the need for sound ethical behavior. Shortfalls in character traits are generally career terminators. The military services have written about and studied extensively the ethics of officership. In 1987 alone, the Army published three new official publications on leadership and related ethical issues.[12] Military and federal courts have acknowledged the special trust, confidence, and responsibility required of military officers.[13] Professional ethics are the most critical aspect of Army leadership; competence in military leadership has a unique ethical dimension.[14] Ethical rules for lawyers who are part of such an environment must take into account such uncommon ethical demands.

Military life is carried on in a closely structured, cloistered environment, and the concern of military leaders for morality, self-sacrifice and the justness of their cause has an almost ecclesiastical quality. The institutional concern for ethical behavior and a plethora of standards of conduct, military service policies, procedures, orders, regulations, laws, and an officer's oath to the Constitution—all designed to protect against abuse of powers—stake out a well-marked trail around many behavioral pitfalls. The law channels professional choices for the military to a greater degree than for many in the private sector. Even in combat, laws of armed conflict and rules of engagement shape military decisions.

The high degree of structure in the military is not surprising. The basic military mission carries with it a higher demand for ethical accountability. In the midst of democracy, military leaders are entrusted with an autocratic power to direct, to judge, to punish, to restrict liberty, and to send others to their deaths, if necessary. Military leaders at the higher levels have the potential to influence decisions that affect our very survival as a nation. Most soldiers are comfortable with both their commitment to soldiering and their oath to support the Constitution, notwithstanding the perceptions of some military commentators who are troubled by "careerism," loss of "warrior spirit," or inadequate appreciation of constitutional principles.[15]

ETHICAL RULES FOR STAFF JUDGE ADVOCATE AND COMMAND RELATIONS

With an abundance of rules, standards, customs, and laws already guiding military officers in their conduct, and with civilian professional rules of ethics already applicable to lawyers, one might ask why it is necessary to promulgate yet another such rule. The short answer, already suggested, is that the staff judge advocate to commander relationship has unique aspects because both parties owe allegiance to the Constitution and the governmental hierarchy as long as they hold their offices. The relationship between staff judge advocates and commanders involves a duality of purpose, at times intimate and personal, at other times structured and formal. With the mingling of professional and personal factors, a potential exists for misunderstandings. It is, therefore, useful to have norms for dealing with unethical as well as unlawful acts. Role clarification provides additional safeguards for the government, additional deterrence for the potential lawbreaker, additional assistance for staff judge advocates representing the Army acting through its agents, and proper representation for the aberrational commander who could persist in an illegal action.

Inherent in the staff judge advocate to commander relationship is a more fundamental ethical issue: the extent to which laws and codes can change ethical attitudes. What is beyond serious dispute is that ethical thought and careful formulation of ethical standards have a salutary or positive effect on action.[16] Setting down what is and what is not acceptable increases ethical awareness and sensitivity. Objective standards cut against our human tendencies to rationalize actions to support purely personal benefits. Knowing that there are rules, sanctions for violations, and effective enforcement procedures, most of us reduce our incidents of misconduct, whether due to heightened ethical consciousness and internal motivation to act ethically or to a more pragmatic concern for self-preservation.

Most military officers reach an easy acceptance of basic ethical standards of behavior. One does not survive without a well-developed ethical consciousness. The trick is applying the theoretical standards to subtle, real world scenarios, where rights and wrongs are not always neatly discernible, choices are limited to degrees of imperfection, and reasonable compromises are sometimes the only way to participate meaningfully. Hence, notwithstanding the general agreement of all military officers on common ethical and legal norms, opinions often vary on how to apply those norms in practical decisionmaking. To the extent that there is controversy over the application of ethical norms among senior leaders, the case is strengthened for more ethical study and the formulation of well-considered guidelines that reflect realistic standards of ethical behavior. With these thoughts in mind, the need for ethical standards designed specifically for legal practice in the military is more apparent.

THE STAFF JUDGE ADVOCATE-COMMAND-ARMY RELATIONSHIP

Official military justice guidance, rule 1.13, provides that Army lawyers, other than those who are specifically assigned to individual defense or legal assistance duties, represent the Department of the Army "acting through its authorized officials." "Authorized officials" include "commanders of armies, corps and divisions," and the heads of other Army activities, such as installation commanders.[17] The confidential, lawyer-client relationship that exists between a command lawyer and the Army client may extend to commanders, so long as the commander acts lawfully on behalf of the Army and the matters discussed with the command lawyer relate to official Army business.[18]

The attorney-client privilege encourages full and free communications between an attorney and a client by requiring the attorney to keep in confidence information relating to the representation. An attorney may not disclose such information except as authorized by applicable rules of professional conduct. Typically, disclosures are authorized to avert certain crimes or frauds on the court and as appro-

DENNIS F. COUPE

priate for proper representation. Hence, identifying the client, whether it is an organization or an individual agent of the organization, is crucial to attachment of the privilege.

If a staff judge advocate becomes aware that a commander is engaged or has engaged in illegal command action or intends to take illegal action knowingly in a situation reasonably imputable to the Army, the staff judge advocate must proceed "in the best interests of the Army." Measures that staff judge advocates should consider when facing these unusual situations include (1) advising the commander of the potential illegality and the conflict with Army interests; (2) asking the commander to reconsider; (3) requesting permission to seek a separate legal opinion or decision on the matter; and (4) making a referral to the legal authority in the next higher command.[19]

No identical provision to Army as client relations, as in rule 1.13, exists in private sector ethical codes, although the duties of a corporate counsel to the stockholders rather than the corporate officers is somewhat analogous.[20] Army guidance is based on the well-established, fundamental notion that the true client of command lawyers is the Army in the first instance and ultimately the laws and government of the United States. Three related tenets are involved: (1) the sworn duty of all Army officers to support the Constitution and the system of laws and government expressed therein; (2) the extension of our constitutional allegiance to the U.S. Army, through the Department of Defense and the Executive branch; and (3) the recognition that our ultimate loyalties to the Constitution, public service, and our at-large government employer must prevail over any conflicting personal interests that may arise.

The significance of Army as client guidance lies more in what rule 1.13 says about the tripartite staff judge advocate-commander-Army relationship than in the guidance provided on how to cope with aberrational[21] cases of intentionally illegal conduct by senior commanders. Regarding the lawyer-client relationship, rule 1.13 states:

> When a judge advocate or other Army lawyer is . . . designated to provide legal services to the head [commander] of the organization, the lawyer-client relationship exists between the lawyer and the Army as represented by the head [commander] of the organization as to matters within the scope of the official business of the organization. The head [commander] of the organization *may not invoke the lawyer-client privilege or the rule of confidentiality* for the [commander's] own benefit but may invoke either for the benefit of the Army. In so invoking . . . on behalf of the Army, the [commander] is subject to being overruled by higher authority in the Army [emphasis added].[22]

The comment to rule 1.13 elaborates on the relationship:

> The Army and its commands, units, and activities are legal entities, but cannot act except through their authorized officers. . . . [A] judge advocate . . . normally represents the *Army acting through its officers.* . . . It is to that client when acting as a representative of the organization that a lawyer's immediate professional obligation and responsibility exists [emphasis added].[23]

The comment goes on to say that official lawyer-commander communications are protected by confidentiality (rule 1.5), but the comment contains the following words of caution: "This does not mean, however, that the officer . . . is a *client of the lawyer. It is the Army, and not the officer . . . which benefits from Rule 1.6 confidentiality."*[24]

Prior to promulgation of Army as client guidance, rule 1.13, and the Army *Rules of Professional Conduct for Lawyers*, there was no clear statutory, regulatory, or ethical guidance defining the nature of staff judge advocates-commander-Army relationships in terms of client loyalty and privilege from disclosure.[25] Few problems arose because a high degree of professionalism characterized relationships between staff judge advocates and senior commanders. Occasionally, however, confusion arose from loose distinctions between personal and institutional loyalties, and between a right to *privacy* for personal disclosures or secrets, and protected lawyer-client *privileges*. A distinction should be and is drawn by Army guidance between opinion or thoughts that *should* not be disclosed, as a matter of personal privacy that are no one else's business, and what *must* be disclosed as required by law and by our paramount duty to the government. Ambiguous language in a now rescinded Department of Army pamphlet[26] contributed to the mistaken notion among some that a staff judge advocate's loyalty to a commander ought to be an all-or-nothing, undivided, right-or-wrong commitment, to the exclusion of other loyalties, just as attorney-client loyalties are often described. Of course, limits exist on the duties and loyalties of lawyers to their clients, whether personal or institutional. Representation of any client must be zealous but within ethical and legal bounds.[27]

As critical as personal loyalty and freedom of expression are to a successful staff judge advocate-commander relationship, there should be no confusion that such expression extends to counsel for clearly illegal actions taken or to nondisclosure for illegal action to be taken. Defense counsel should handle the former case, higher authority the latter. The proposition that loyalty to a personal interest (in the form of a privilege from disclosure) is an *absolute* requirement that should properly prevail over loyalty to the law has been so thoroughly rejected that it bears little discussion.[28] In his book, *Limits of Loyalty*, A. C. Wedemyer describes the predicament facing many senior German officers in World War II:

> Colonel General Beck . . . General Rommel and thousands of other patriotic Germans in the military service were . . . torn between loyalties to those in power and their innate loyalties to principles of decency and justice. . . . [T]here was a duty, in Rommel's view . . . of loyalty to the nation which now came into conflict with the duty to the commander.[29]

General George Marshall went a step further: "[A]n officer's ultimate, commanding loyalty at all times is to his country and not to his service or superiors."[30] Similarly, the "Code of Ethics for Government Service" in Army Regulation 600-50 states, "Any person in Government service should *a.* Put loyalty . . . to country above loyalty to persons . . . [and] *b.* Uphold the Constitution, laws and regulations of the United States . . . ever conscious that public office is a public trust."[31] The courts, as have the great majority of commanders, recognize these same principles as applicable to military officers.[32]

Occasional confusion over attorney-client privilege and the appropriate object of a command lawyer's loyalty made it apparent that ethical "rules of engagement" for lawyers needed to be precisely defined. Informality and trust had to be preserved, without protecting known, deliberate illegal acts. Implicit in Army guidance is the requirement that both commanders and their staff judge advocates, as representatives of the Army, obey their fiduciary duties to the law and honor their oaths to the Constitution. So long as this duty is met and there is the recognition that public office equates to a public trust that the offices will be exercised lawfully, commanders are entitled to expect both confidentiality and loyalty from their lawyers. Whether the Army extends that confidence to commanders as "quasiclients"[33] of the command lawyer or simply as protection for matters conveyed in the expectation of privacy, staff judge advocates have an ethical duty not to disclose such communications to those who have no legitimate right to know. The fact that the Army and the government and, when relevant to trial issues, opposing counsel and the courts have a right to know of evidence of illegalities or conflicts of interest does not detract from but bolsters the professionalism of the relationship.

"HE TELLS ME EVERYTHING, AND THAT'S THE WAY I WANT IT"

Of course, commanders have a right to expect that their staff judge advocates will "keep them out of trouble" and respect a *limited* rather than an absolute confidentiality of communications. Army military justice guidance does not affect this situation. "Inadvertent" illegality is distinguished from deliberate illegality. But if some boundaries or "good faith" of the staff judge advocate commander representation are not well established, a commander may expect his own personal legal representation and strict confidentiality from the staff judge advocate, vis-a-vis the government. When the staff judge advocate does not provide this representation, the commander may sense that the lawyer is merely attempting to avoid association with the commander in the commander's hour of need. Clear rules and bilateral understanding of those rules at the outset should minimize any such misunderstandings.

The drafters of the Army as client guidance of rule 1.13 understood that commanders must have the support of their lawyers and must be free to discuss with their staff judge advocates any aspect of official business fully, frankly, and with the assurance of confidentiality, except as to those higher authorities who have legitimate right to disclosure. The comment to the rule 1.13 states, "When the officers . . . make decisions for the Army, the decisions ordinarily must be accepted by the lawyer even if their utility or prudence is doubtful. Decisions concerning policy and operations, including ones entailing serious risk, are not as such in the lawyer's province."[34] Thus, Army military justice guidance changes nothing of substance. Rule 1.13 merely clarifies an area of potential misunderstanding and provides a structure for addressing representational conflicts. No well-intentioned commander need hesitate to discuss any command option, power, or duty with the staff judge advocate. Providing advice on such matters is the bread and butter of the staff judge advocate's job. Subject to the narrow exceptions required by law and the ethical rules for governmental access to the information as described above, no third party disclosures of a commander's private communications are appropriate. Only a clearly intended or actual illegality that might be imputed to the Army or a violation of a legal obligation to the Army is to be disclosed. Only those who insist upon proceeding against these Army interests lose their derivative protection from disclosure.

Staff judge advocates facing a situation where a command is engaged in illegal action may refer the matter to or ask for guidance from higher authority in the technical chain. This provision of Army military justice guidance reflects a right that already exists in article 6(b), UCMJ.

The same basic principle that governs staff judge advocate-commander relationships also applies to subordinate command representatives and other command lawyers. If these officials insist upon illegal action and cannot otherwise be deterred, the situation should be brought to the attention of the higher commander or supervising command lawyer.

The Army rules integrate, cross reference, and extend the Army as client provisions of rule 1.13 in several of the other rules, wherever appropriate to clarify the nature of the ethical duty described. The comment in rule 1.4, "Communication," requires that appropriate Army officials be kept informed in legal developments on behalf of the Army client. The comment to rule 1.6, "Confidentiality of Information," notes that lawyers who represent the Army may inquire within the Army to clarify the possible need for withdrawal from representation of local officials where doubt exists about contemplated criminal conduct. Rule 1.7, "Conflict of Interest," includes the following in its comment:

> Loyalty is an essential element in the lawyer's relationship to a client. . . . [L]oyalty to a client is . . . impaired when a lawyer cannot consider, recommend or carry out an appropriate course of action for the client because of the lawyer's other responsibilities or interests . . .

> A client including an organization (see rule 1.13b), may consent to representation notwithstanding a conflict.[35]

Similarly, rule 5.4, "Professional Independence of a Lawyer," requires a lawyer to exercise individual professional judgment in representing a client, free of competing influences and loyalties. The comment to rule 8.5, "Jurisdiction," applies Army military justice guidance to the separate roles of lawyers, whether serving the Army as an institutional client or serving individual clients as authorized by the Army.

Judge advocates and other Army lawyers are both commissioned officers and "officers of the court," with complementing, but not identical, ethical obligations in each capacity. Army military justice guidance is partially analogous to American Bar Association and Federal Bar Association guidance on duties of civilian attorneys to their corporate or institutional employers.[36] As in the evidentiary privilege rationale of Military Rule of Evidence 502,[37] "lawyer-client privilege," Army military justice guidance recognizes that the client can be a public entity and entitled, as such, to claim the privilege of nondisclosure of confidential communications of its representatives.

The greatest value of the Army as client guidance of rule 1.13 is its clarification of respective, official roles and of legal relationships that are occa-

---

sionally misunderstood. Public servants, and military authorities in particular, conduct their official business through the power entrusted to them by the government. Commanders and Army lawyers must expect that they may be held accountable for their actions and should conduct their activities accordingly, mindful of potential scrutiny by judges, by higher authorities in all branches of government, and even by the public at large when the information is not protected from disclosure.[38]

CONCLUSION

The Book of Timothy reminds us that laws are not made for the righteous. Yet even for the righteous, the full ethical dimension of decisionmaking is not always obvious. The best of us sometimes fail to realize all the consequences of decisions. All of us can benefit from wise counsel. Well-considered laws and codes of behavior alert us to ethical issues that we may not otherwise perceive, and inform us of societal preferences for resolving conflicting and sometimes ambiguous choices in an increasingly complex world. Wise rules of ethical behavior are beneficial norms, serving as a departure point for subjective and objective analysis, stimulating ethical discussion and thought, and conforming behavior to desirable ends.[39] We learn from the great German philosopher, Immanuel Kant, echoing similar thoughts of Socrates two millenniums earlier, that we should strive to develop good laws and obey them, not because the laws are perfect but because it is our duty and otherwise there is but chaos.[40] Army military justice guidance represents an effort to develop the laws of our profession.

Official duties should be performed lawfully, in a manner that will withstand public scrutiny, even if that scrutiny never occurs. The dictates of law, our oath, and applicable ethical rules must be observed as necessary conditions of public service. Keeping the Army's interests in mind strengthens, rather than detracts from, the commander's entitlement to special care, loyalty, and protection from illegality or unwarranted disclosure. By setting the ground rules out clearly, the Army as client guidance of rule 1.13 fortifies an already sound relationship among staff judge advocates, commanders, and the Army client.

NOTES

1. 52 Fed. Reg. 122 (1987).

2. Department of Army, DA, *Legal Services: Rules of Professional Conduct for Lawyers*, Pamphlet 27-26 (December 31, 1987) [hereinafter in endnotes as Rules]; Army Regulations (AR) 27-10, *Military Justice* (March 18, 1988).

3. The Rules define *lawyer* as "a member of the bar . . . who practices law under the disciplinary jurisdiction of the Judge Advocate General. This includes judge advocates . . . and civilian lawyers practicing before tribunals conducted pursuant to the Uniform Code of Military Justice and the Manual for Courts-Martial. . . . " The Rules define *tribunal* as including "all fact-finding, review or adjudicatory bodies or proceedings convened or initiated pursuant to applicable law." The *Army* is the immediate subagency of the Department of Defense, and Executive agency. This in no respect limits the ultimate duty to the Constitution, the law, and the three branches of the Federal Government.

4. 64 Stat. 120 (May 5, 1950).

5. *Manual for Courts-Martial*, United States, 1969 (Rev. ed.).

6. The Army, Navy, and Marine Corps agreed on the desirability of promulgating ethical rules with specific guidance for military lawyers. However, the Navy/Marine Corps guidance is less comprehensive, includes no commentary, and is inapplicable to civilian lawyers. The Air Force is studying the need for ethical rules tailored to their service practice. The Court of Military Appeals continues to apply the ABA Model Code of Professional Responsibility, per Rule of Court 12(a), 4 M.J.XCV, CI (1977). It is hoped that the Army rules will provide the basis for a more uniform approach among the Services and the court.

7. *See, e.g.*, the "conflict of interest" provisions of 18 U.S.C. s201-209 and the "Ethics in Government" requirements of 5 U.S.C.A. App-I, s201 *et seq* (October 26, 1978; June 13 and 22, 1979). The primary Army authority for investigation of ethical allegations against lawyers is Army Reg. 27-1, *Legal Services: Judge Advocate Legal Service*, para. 5-3) August 1, 1984) (under revision). *See also* Army Reg. 27-10, *Legal Services: Military Justice*, para. 5-8 (July 10, 1987) (under revision); Army Reg. 600-50, *Standards of Conduct*, App. D (September 25, 1986). The Federal Ethical Considerations (F.E.C.) of the Federal Bar Association (FBA) are an excellent source of guidance for the federal sector attorney but are not adapted to military practice. The Army Office of the Judge Advocate General also issues an annual "Reference Guide to Prohibited Activities of Military and Former Military Personnel, as a research tool for judge advocates facing statutory requirements related to common ethical problems.

8. Although the Supreme Court recognized, in Parker v. Levy, 417 U.S. 733, 744 (1973), that "[m]ilitary law is a jurisprudence . . . separate and apart from the law which governs our federal," such differences exist more outside the courtroom than within. See Solorio v. United States, 107 S. Ct. 2924 (1987).

9. Rules, preamble, 2

10. *Id.*

11. *See generally* Frankena, Ethics (2nd ed. 1973), at IX-XI.

12. Department of the Army, *Leadership and Command at Senior Levels*, Field Manual 22-103; Department of the Army,

Executive Leadership (1982), Pam. 600-80; and the *Army Rules of Professional Conduct for Lawyers.*

13. *See, e.g.,* United States v. Means, 20 M.J. 162 (C.M.A. 1981). Chief Judge Everett notes: "In light of the unique special position of honor and trust enjoyed by an officer . . . it is quite understandable why the President determined that an officer should only be sentenced to confinement by the highest military tribunal." *Id.* at 167.

14. *See* Sorley, *Competence as an Ethical Imperative,* Army, August 1982, at 42. Sorely argues persuasively that competence is a virtue that subsumes many others.

15. *See* R. Gabriel, *supra* note 12, at 119-29.

16. See, e.g., Ehrlich, *Common Issues of Professional Responsibility,* The Geo. J. Legal Ethics 41 (1987). Ehrlich points out that forty-one professional societies have developed ethical rules, and notes benefits from comparative analysis. John A. Rohr observes, "Although one might quarrel with certain self-serving aspects of the codes of ethics developed by the medical and legal professions, there is little doubt that it is the high sense of *professional definition* among physicians and lawyers that accounts for the relatively clear ethical standards of their profession." J. Rohr, Ethics for Bureaucrats 10 (1978) (emphasis added). Dean Derek C. Bok is quoted in R. Gabriel, To *Serve With Honor* 9 (1982): "Most men . . . will profit from instruction that helps them become more alert to ethical issues, and to apply their moral values more carefully and vigorously to the ethical dilemmas they encounter in their professional lives."

17. Rule 1.13(a).

18. Disclosures or nondisclosure of confidences may be analyzed from at least four perspectives: (1) what evidence rules or court orders require as a matter of discovery for a fair trial of an accused; (2) what ethical rules require to preserve the confidences of clients; (3) what is required by the Freedom of Information and Privacy Acts, and (4) what is morally required by personal expectation or commitment. Distinguishing disclosure issues according to each of these categories is helpful to analysis of particular questions. Discovery and ethical disclosure obligations are summarized in Department of the Army, Pamphlet 27-173, *Trial Procedure,* paras. 30-5 and 30-6, (February 15, 1987), [hereinafter DA Pam. 27-173]. Multiple clients with conflicting

DENNIS F. COUPE

interests are prohibited by the ABA Code of Professional Responsibility, Canon 5 (1980).

19. Rule 1.13(b) (1)-(4).

20. ABA Model Rule 1.13(b), "Organization as Client" and Federal Ethical Consideration 4-1 of Cannon 4, FBA Rules, were models for Army Rule 1.13 but do not reflect unique aspects of the SJA-commander relationship.

21. In an unpublished report, "Legal operations in the European Theater during World War II, by LTC Joseph W. Riley, U.S. Army, JAGC, it is interesting to note that problems between staff judge advocates and commanders are considered virtually nonexistent. See "Legal Questions Arising in the Theater of Operations," Study No. 87, 1947, (on file in the Army Library, Headquarters, Department of Army).

22. Rule 1.13(a). DA Pam. 17-173, discusses the staff judge advocate commanding general relationship prior to the Rules at para 30-3. In United States v. Albright, 9 C.M.A. 628, 26 C.M.R. 408 (1958), the roles of the SJA were alternatively described as "advisor" on legal matters, "chief spokesman" for the commander, "legal conduit," and wearer of "judicial robes" when reviewing criminal charges and records of trial.

23. Rule 1.13 comment.

24. Ibid.

25. *See* Gaydos, *The SJA as the Commander's Lawyer: A Realistic Proposal, The Army Lawyer,* August 1983, at 14.

26. Department of the Army, *Staff Judge Advocate Handbook,* Pamphlet 27-5, para. 19b (July 1963). "He [the commander] does want a legal advisor whose loyalty is unquestioned." *Id.*

27. Model Code of Professional Responsibility, Canon 7 (1980); ABA Model Rules of Professional Conduct 1.6 and 3.3 *See also,* Nix v. Whiteside, 106 S. Ct. 988 (1986); Hazard, *Nature of Legal Ethics,* 1 Geo J. Legal Ethics 43, 1987, 67-84. Prof. Hazard makes a persuasive case that the ABA Model Rules on confidentiality (1.6) represents an unsuccessful attempt "to create an island of refuse in the legal sea of integrity and to establish a pirate's cove of confidentiality." *Id.* at 67. For this and other reasons, the Army Rules impose a clearer duty upon attorneys to disclose future crime under Rules 1.6, 1.13 and 3.3, than exists under the ABA Model Rules. Hazard also makes a compelling argument that the conduct of a client is "the ultimate source

of ethical issues for a lawyer." *Id.* at 84. According to Hazard, unless there is ethical association with the legal actions of a client, "the administration of law becomes a sporting contest . . . with lawyers manufacturing rights for clients that do not exist and erasing duties that do." *Id.* at 83. *But see* Wasserstrom, *Lawyers as Professionals*, 5 Hum. Rights L. Rev. 1 (1975) for a contrary view. The question of how to deal with client perjury under the Rules is addressed in O'Hare, *supra* note 13.

28. *See e.g.*, J. Sorley, "Duty, Honor, Country: Practice and Precept," in M. Wakin, *War, Morality and the Military Profession*, 2d ed. (1986). ("The essence is loyalty . . . to ideals that transcend self.") *Accord*, Philip Flammer, *Conflicting Loyalties and the American Military Ethic*, in M. Wakin, *supra*, at 165. ("[T]he military ethic calls for ultimate loyalty . . . to ideals that transcend self.") *Accord*, Philip Flammer, *Conflicting Loyalties and the American Military Ethic*, in M. Wakin, *supra*, at 165. ("[T]he military ethic calls for ultimate loyalty to cause and principles higher than self . . . loyalty demands aa firm will to justice and truth.") Wakin himself observes, "It is no longer the case that extreme value is placed on personal loyalty to a commander; that aspect of military honor is transferred to the oath of office which requires allegiance to the Constitution." M. Wakin, *supra*, at 185. *See also* Reese, *An officer's Oath*, 25 Mil. L. Rev. 1 (1964).

29. A. C. Wedmeyer, Limits of Loyalty 125 (1980).

30. R. Gabriel, "To Serve With Honor," supra note 12.

31. Department of the Army, *Standards of Conduct*, Army Reg. 600-50, App. D (September 26, 1986).

32. *See, e.g.*, United States v. Scott, 21 M.J. 345 (C.M.A. 1986). Commenting on article 133, UCMJ, ("conduct unbecoming"), Judge Cox states in his concurring opinion: "It [article 133] focuses on the fact that an accused is 'an officer' and that his conduct has brought discredit upon all officers and, thus, upon the honor, integrity, and good character inherent in that important, unique status." *Id.* at 351 (Cox, J., concurring).

33. The term "quasi-client" is attributed to G.C. Hazard, Jr., in *Ethics in the Practice of Law*, J. Hum. Rights (Fall 1978), p. 44. Prof. Hazard also provides a useful model for analysis of the SJA-Commander-Army relationship in *Triangular Lawyer Relationships: An Exploratory Analysis, Geo. J. Legal Ethics (1987)*. The term "derivative client" also has been used.

34. Rule 1.13 comment.

35. Rule 1.7 comment.

36. *See* notes 7, 13 and 30, *supra*.

37. M.R.E. 502, Manual for Courts-Martial, United States, 1984, Mil R. Evid. 502.

38. "Interagency" communications and attorney-client predecisional memoranda are generally exempt from mandatory disclosure under the Freedom of Information Act, 5 U.S.C. 552(b) (5) (1982).

39. "Our central problem is . . . an obtuseness in refusing to see basic choices among incompatible ends [when we are] unable to agree on normal or prudential norms." Liebman, *Legislating Morality in the Proposed CIA Charter*, in Public Duties: The Moral Obligations of Government Officials, 248 (1982). The editors of the *Georgetown Journal of Legal Ethics*, note: "The need for considered reflection about the ethical issues lawyers confront in daily practice is great." 1 Geo. L. J. Legal Ethics ii (1987). R. B. Stewart, in *Reformation of American Administrative Law*, 88 Harv. L. Rev. 8, 28 (1985), notes that the "astonishing capacity for rationalization" that exists when professional environments are left "morally ambiguous."

40. I. Kant, "In Critique of Practical Reason" (1788) summarized in 4 *The Encyclopedia of Philosophy*, 317-22 (967). *See* W.B. Gallie, *Philosopher of Peace and War* 36-58 (1978).

LIMITS OF
LOYALTY AND OBEDIENCE:
DOES THE
MILITARY PHYSICIAN
SERVE TWO MASTERS?

EUGENE G. LAFORET
Captain, Marine Corps, U.S.N.R.

Captain Laforet describes confidentiality and other issues in which traditional doctor-patient loyalties may come into conflict with the military obligations of a uniformed officer-physician. Captain Laforet notes that all physicians [like all service members?] must deal with ethical conflicts, and he maintains that one must have an "informed conscience" to resolve those conflicts.

No man can serve two masters. For either he will hate the one and love the other; or he will sustain the one and despise the other.

—MATTHEW 6:24

For two millennia and more, physicians in the West have tended to assert the primacy of the individual patient over and against the claims of institutions or of societies. But clearly, tensions have always existed in this order of things, more wrenching at some times than at others. And in no milieu is this potential conflict more obvious than, perhaps, in that of military medicine. Even the seeming synonyms, "military physician" and "physician in the military" bespeak a certain bias as to perceived roles. Am I primarily "military" or primarily "physician"?

SPECIFIC DIFFICULTIES

Confidentiality. Confidentiality, it would seem, is an area in which the professional ethical strictures imposed on the civilian physician may commonly be abrogated in the military, but on reflection it becomes apparent that confidentiality has never been an absolute value in civilian medicine nor has it been ignored in the military. Civilian physicians are required by law to report certain communicable diseases to public health authorities and injuries such as gunshot wounds to the police. Similarly, the military flight surgeon is required to report medical unfitness for flying status to the operational commander. These situations are not, strictly speaking, violations of patient confidentiality, since the action is essentially predetermined and generally known. There is therefore little distinction in these instances between the loyalty and obedience required institutionally of the military physician and that demanded by society of his civilian counterpart. In fact, the military patient's perception of his military physician as a member of the same organization with obvious responsibilities to the organization thereto—both wear a uniform and possession of a military rank— may make issues of confidentiality less opaque than in civilian medicine, where the demands of certain third parties for confidential information may not be suspected by the patient. But, despite evolving experience,[1] ambiguities are inevitable, and the medical officer can draw neither comfort nor guidance from these concluding words of D.D. Knoll:

> The military physician should be aware of the absence of a doctor-patient privilege in military law, and should be cautious in his assurances to his patients that the information they may divulge to him will be kept confidential. His ethical duty not to reveal the secrets of his patient is still applicable to his practice, but must give way to his official duties as a military officer when the two are in conflict and a clear legal obligation requires him to speak.[2]

And what of thornier issues of confidentiality in military medicine? May a commander demand personal information of a general nature about subordinates that was garnered in the course of a psychiatric interview? No more than in civilian life, unless authorized beforehand by the patient. Note that I evade the issue of breaking a professional confidence if the physician acquires information of a potential threat to others[3]. As a nonpsychiatrist I do not often encounter such difficulties, and as a physician interested in medical ethics I have not resolved the dilemma to my own satisfaction. But the point is that, in general, the professional ethics related to confidentiality in the military are quite similar to those encountered in the civilian sector. As Hundert states:

> Examples in which doctors are forced to act as "double agents" (as when psychiatrists are called on by society to protect society from dangerous mentally ill people and not just serve their patients) highlight the difference between morality in the narrow and broad senses, *but these levels of complexity are always operating* [italics mine].[4]

The basic concept of medical confidentiality—once deemed as sacred and inviolable as the seal of the confession is for priests—has continued to erode as Western medicine loses its roots. This is not necessarily a greater problem in military medicine than elsewhere, but its potential for becoming so must be recognized. For instance, some evidence suggests that military personnel are more trusting of the confidentiality of civilian physicians than of military physicians. A military authorized study of twenty military personnel with human immunodeficiency virus (HIV) infection found that only 20 percent were homosexual or bisexual.[5] Examiners concluded that heterosexual transmission was much commoner than has been appreciated. However, in subsequent interviews by civilian case-investigators 70 percent of the subjects admitted to being homosexual or bisexual.[6] Rightly or wrongly, therefore, it would seem that military personnel may view the military physician as renouncing the professional ethic of confidentiality in favor of loyalty and obedience to the organization. If this is so, this misperception requires renewed emphasis on confidentiality of medical information by both medical officers and, perhaps *a fortiori*, by line officers.

Medical Evaluations for Administrative Purposes. Medical evaluations for administrative purposes also test the limits of loyalty and obedience of military medical professionals. A commander may find that getting a troublesome individual out of his unit may be accomplished more easily and expeditiously on medical grounds rather than by administrative means. Needless to say, a medical officer who permits himself to be suborned in this fashion is in violation of basic professional ethics. But this example is fortunately uncommon. Of more moment is the subject of psychiatric evaluations for administrative purposes. Here, it would seem, the physician can easily become a double agent unless he is aware of the possibility and has sufficient ethical mettle to resist. According to E.K. Jeffer, "the entire effort is to create a situation where commander, psychiatrist, and soldier are united in a common effort to find the best possible solution". Jeffer concludes,

> Psychiatrists are frequently called upon to evaluate individuals for judicial or administrative purposes. These evaluations are frequently seen as an invalid area for psychiatric expertise, or as an uncomfortable and unrewarded necessary evil. The author has found that, within the military, the utilization of an active consultation model for administrative evaluations allows for a positive and productive involvement in the administrative process. Additionally, the development of reporting vehicles, which combine the psychiatric and legal vocabularies, enhances the consultative role and diminishes misunderstandings and unnecessary adversary confrontations. In the military, administrative evaluations can become the first step in primary prevention consultation.[7]

And though J.P. Morgan does not accept the inevitability of yielding to the bureaucracy, he is less sanguine than Jeffer that such a conflict of interest can be resolved ethically by the military physician:

> The physician who accepts payment for his services from an institution rather than from the patient may have some conflicts, but his independence and professional judgment may remain unchanged vis-a-vis the patient. . . . But as the bureaucratic nature (and power over the physician) of the organization increases, such independence is much more difficult to achieve. He may often become the captive of his employer and find it more difficult to justify what he does as service to the patient. The military psychiatrist often falls into this latter group.[8]

The Military Physician versus the Military Health-Care Bureaucracy. After a long latent period that some would describe as typical, the fiscal constraints of today's medical technology have finally been recognized by the military health-care bureaucracy. In essence, optimal medical care for the individual is pitted against the monetary resources of the medical department. And needless to say, the latter competes in turn with the many nonmedical entities of the organization that it serves. Resolving the resultant tension is the proper concern of bureaucracies, but I am concerned with the role of the *individual* military physician. Moral decisions can be made only by an individual moral agent and not by committees. Both peer review and utilization review have been implemented to address the fiscal constraints of modern health care. These reviews have produced value conflicts for the individual practitioner but also "have become institutionalized in the military medical system."

> It seems clear that whatever solutions are tried, they must include a sensitivity to the basic value system that permeates medicine. Any proposed solution that is inconsistent with this value system will founder. Clinicians can no longer practice within the military medical setting with a blithe disregard for fiscal constraints, and rightly so. However, in the pressure to bring . . . medical costs under control, we must remain aware of some of the basic value conflicts. . . . It would seem that both the clinicians and the monitors of health-care delivery must develop some knowledge of the tenets of each other's creed and be prepared to accept some compromises in their value systems in the search for solutions.[9]

In the arena of health care costs, then, there would seem to be some limits to the loyalty and obedience demanded of the military physician by his organization. No one, however—at least at this juncture—is willing to offer a precise delineation of these limits. And perhaps wisely so. Some tensions are resolved by a rupture.

THE FINAL ARBITER

An eleven-point code, "Ethics and Professional Relationships," for health-care practitioners in the military was made available to the Committee on Medical Ethics in the Military at the November 1985 meeting of the Society of Medical Consultants to the Armed Forces.[10] Virtually all of the statements in this code, as in most similar compilations, are bland generalities to which no reasonable person could object. But "Principle 11" raises a significant difficulty. Principle 11 reads: "Government service or employment, as a public trust, requires that the health-care practitioner place loyalty to country, ethical principles, and law above private gain and other interests." Fair enough, as far as it goes. But the assumption is that country, ethical principles, and law are always in harmony. Only a moment's reflection shows that this is not necessarily the case. Posterity, both in and out of medicine, has never managed to forgive those Nazi physicians whose loyalty and obedience to country and law superseded that to the long-established ethical principles of their profession. But where *does* one turn when such a collision is inescapable and one must act? Despite its negation by many modern philosophers and psychologists, conscience—an *informed* conscience—must remain the final arbiter of individual moral behavior in such situations.

When the military physician's duty of loyalty and obedience conflicts with his ethical standards he is morally obligated to adhere to the later. In most instances of this nature some accommodation—compromise is too value-laden a term—is reached. But when one side or the other or both remain adamant, confrontation is inevitable and the conclusion preordained. In a well-publicized Vietnam-era case, Captain Howard B. Levy was court-martialed for his refusal on grounds of conscience to provide medical training to nonmedical Special Force troops for use in Vietnam.[11] Prescinding or abstracting from such ancillary issues as politicization of the medical enterprise, rejection of proffered alternatives, possibly confused data base, and ethical scrupulosity, the right of Captain Levy to reach his personal moral decision was in full accord with traditional medical ethics[12]. He set *his* limits of loyalty and obedience . . . but the Army did not concur.

Other military physicians in other milieux have adapted in other ways to the potential conflict between the requirement of loyalty and obedience to the organization and that of adherence to one's moral principles. Edward M. Colbach, a Berry Plan psychiatrist, reported for active duty during the Vietnam war despite his strong reservations about its moral legitimacy. He shortly found himself in Vietnam as a combat psychiatrist. There his twelve-month tour included participation in Medical Civil Action Patrols (MED CAPS), an experience that "degraded whatever medical ethic I still held onto" and that "certainly was demeaning of the Hippocratic

Oath." Based as they are on his service as a combat psychiatrist, his views on the limits of loyalty and obedience are particularly cogent:

[I] . . . have always believed that there probably is such a thing as a just war. St. Augustine and St. Thomas Aquinas first defined this. Essentially a just war is one that is initiated by legitimate authority with good intentions and for a good cause. War should be waged only as a last resort and always with the most limited means. Whether the Vietnam conflict fits these criteria or not is really beyond me to say. I did accept that as a just war when I agreed to serve in it.[13]

And once having acquiesced to my role as a military psychiatrist, I then had to accept that my obligation to my individual patient was far superseded by my obligation to the military and, eventually, to my country. This focus is the main ethic of military psychiatry.

Finally, brief mention must be made of biological warfare research, an area that necessarily involves physicians but which seems the very antithesis of the healing ethic. The distinction between "offensive" (and therefore morally unacceptable) and "defensive" (and therefore morally acceptable) biological warfare is a specious one that does not alter the ethical equation. One might legitimately argue—though I do not—that to require a military physician to participate in such endeavors would exceed acceptable limits of loyalty and obedience.[14] Other targeted research, such as that relating to sickle cell trait in healthy military personnel, has less obvious ethical dimensions but could still pose a moral dilemma for some physicians in the armed forces.[15]

CONCLUSION

As with the practice of medicine in general, military medicine may occasion ethical conflicts for the physician. These generally derive from tensions between the rights of the individual patient and those of the organization to which he belongs. Even in the military—or perhaps *especially* in the military—there are limits to the loyalty and obedience that the organization may demand of the physician. Analogous limits are seen in the civilian sector. Although medical ethical conflicts are inevitable in the military as elsewhere, they may be minimized by fostering an understanding of their origins and a program for their resolution. An informed conscience remains the final arbiter of any individual moral decision and—for the military physician—defines the limits of his loyalty and obedience.

NOTES

1. J.R. Morris, "Right Warnings in the Military: an Article 31(b) Update," *Military Law Rev* 115 (Winter 1987): 261-94.

2. D.D. Knoll, "The Physician-Patient Privilege, Article 31, and the Military Doctor," *Military Medicine* 136 (July 1971): 640-43.

3. *Tarasoff v. Board of Regents of the University of California.* 17 Cal. 3d 425; 551 Pac. 2d 334, 131 Cal. Rptr. 14 (1975); S.L. Auster, "Confidentiality in Military Medicine," *Military Medicine* 150: (July 1985): 341-450.

4. E.M. Hundert, "A Model for Ethical Problem Solving in Medicine, with Practical Applications," *American Journal of Psychiatry* (July 1987): 839-46.

LIMITS OF LOYALTY AND OBEDIENCE

5. R.R. Redfield, P.D. Markham, S.Z. Salahuddin, *et al.*, "Heterosexually Acquired HTLV-III/LAV Disease (AIDS-Related Complex and AIDS): Epidemiologic Evidence for Female-to-Male Transmission," *Journal of the American Medical Association* 254 (1985): 2094-96.

6. J.J. Potterat, L. Phillips, J.B. Muth, "Lying to Military Physicians About Risk Factors for HIV Infections,"(corresp.) *Journal of the American Medical Association* 257 (3 April 1987): 1727.

7. E.K. Jeffer, "Psychiatric Evaluations for Administrative Purposes," *Military Medicine* 144 (August 1979): 526-28.

8. J.P. Morgan, "Military Psychiatry—Service to the Mission," *New Physician* 20 (August 1971): 512-18.

9. F.L. Giordano, "Values Conflict in Utilization Review in the Military," *Military Medicine* 150 (April 1985): 221-22.

10. *Ethics and Professional Relations*, Code of conduct for health-care practitioners in federal service.

11. E. Langer, "The Court-Martial of Captain Levy: Medical Ethics v. Military Law," *Science* 156 (9 June 1967): 1346-50; R. Liberman, W. Gold, V.W. Sidel, "Medical Ethics and the Military," *New Physician* 17 (November 1968): 299-309.

12. R.T. Jensen, "Another View of Medical Ethics and the Military," *New Physician* 20 (August 1971): 505-11; E.A. Vastyan, "Warriors in White: Some Questions about the Nature and Mission of Military Medicine," *Texas Report on Biology & Medicine* 6 (Summer 1963): 512-23.

13. E.M. Colbach, "Ethical Issues in Combat Psychiatry," *Military Medicine* 150 (May 1985): 256-65.

14. T. Rosebury, "Medical Ethics and Biological Warfare," *Perspectives on Biology & Medicine* 6 (Summer 1963); 512-23; D. Crozier, "The Physician and Biological Warfare," *New England Journal of Medicine* 284 (6 May 1971): 1008-11.

15. E.G. Howe, III, J.A. Kark, D.G. Wright, "Studying Sickle Cell Trait in Healthy Army Recruits: Should the Research Be Done?" *Clinical Research* 31 (April 1983): 119-25.

INTELLIGENCE COLLECTION AND ANALYSIS: DILEMMAS AND DECISIONS

JOHN B. CHOMEAU
ANNE C. RUDOLPH
Central Intelligence Agency

Chomeau and Rudolph consider the requirement for clandestine operations and covert operations, observing that these operations routinely involve deception and other activities which would in most contexts be considered both illegal and immoral. The authors argue that "just war" principles provide an appropriate ethical framework for such activities.

To establish a consensus for discussion of the intelligence profession as similar to or distinct from other professions, and to assist us in arguing for the importance of a professional ethic, we define *profession* as an honorific title founded on a unique competence in the performance of special tasks or services with a commitment to community-related services which establishes a professional-client relationship.

The intelligence officer is a highly trained professional with strict standards for performance, conduct, and promotion within the profession. Through additional training and overseas travel the intelligence professional is obligated to improve skills in the clandestine collection and analysis of secret information, while always mindful of the responsibility of being a public servant. We assert that the source of an ethical dilemma of keeping secrets in an open, democratic society resides in an unclear notion of who is our client, particularly if circumstances merit security classification of intelligence information. Therefore, we must ponder whether the need to maintain secrecy overrides the right of the American public for an accounting of our activities. As professional intelligence officers we must know for whom we are acting as a moral agent and what secrecy does to change the nature of the professional-client relationship in the sphere of national security affairs?

It is the view of the professional intelligence officer that our clients are ultimately the American people, but in the day-to-day effort to get our jobs done, few have an opportunity to reflect upon this. Under our system of government the congressional oversight panels and the existence of a free press serve as protectors of the public's interest. Accountability for intelligence operations should be ensured through this reflection on the nation's conscience. We must also consider the special responsibility of the intelligence officer as one who is obliged to work in secret, obliged to perfect the skills of the profession, and to employ these skills solely for the benefit of the American society or client. Some of the skills of the professional intelligence officer if exercised outside of their proper purpose or place would be both illegal and immoral. Moreover, the purpose and unique expertise of the intelligence officer is not too dissimilar from the military officer. Both professionals employ skills that have little direct application outside of government. Both support policymakers by managing the use of force in an effort to ensure peace by protecting information and operations vital to our national security. In a sentence, the intelligence professional, like the military officer, protects innocents against aggression.

The fundamental question remains, how does ethics relate to the intelligence profession? After all, it is clear that intelligence officers are supposed to be ethical. That the Intelligence Community has an ethically responsible task is also clear. However, how ethics relates to the specifics of their work and what an individual officer needs to know about ethics is not clear. This issue is not talked about much in the Intelligence Community probably because the "business" of intelligence is shrouded by secrecy, need-to-know, distrust, and deception. Perhaps some prefer the role of ethics in international affairs to be "as little as possible."

When attempting to set forth a body of principles for the conduct of intelligence operations and the inculcation of these principles for officers serving in the collection and analysis components of organizations such as the CIA, one is faced almost immediately with several key questions.

Are there general moral principles governing the conduct of professional intelligence officers? Do we have a code of ethics similar to those which apply to other professions such as law, medicine, and the military? If so, whence do they come, how well are they understood by intelligence officers, and how do we teach them to those involved in collection, analysis, covert action, and the management of intelligence operations? If there is not a recognized code governing the conduct of intelligence operations, in what manner are limits set on what is acceptable and needed, and how do we prevent our profession from accepting guidelines such as "the end does justify the means" or "everything goes, just so you don't get caught?"

Our intent is to present the nature of this question, to describe the moral vitality and bankruptcy of various theoretical approaches to this problem, and to devise a systematic means of processing an ethical question which can be taught to the practitioners of this profession. We assume the intelligence profession possesses power in the form of secret information and this represents a kind of force that can be used to protect our nation's interests. We therefore advocate the application of just war theory as a way of establishing certain prima facie evidence against the use of force in secret intelligence operations until such an act of force may be justified under these criteria. We therefore assert deontological principles against intervention and the use of secrecy except in justifiable cases. Hence the burden of proof is on the consequentialist who must reasonably justify a divergence from the deontological principles by applying the just war criteria. Where possible and within the limits of security we will provide case studies representative of the types of dilemmas that may confront the intelligence professional.

ARGUMENTS

There are several hypothetical arguments that can be made on the issues of whether there exists a body of ethics governing intelligence operations. These arguments will provide a structure for further discussion of the dilemmas.

Our actions are first governed by U.S. law, although some of these statutes were written in such a way that they are subject to a broad interpretation. To deal with these statutes, CIA seeks assistance from its own legal staff, as well as from the Department of Justice and other governmental bodies. A review of intelligence law indicates, however, that it is difficult to derive a moral standard from this source. Many situations are deliberately left fuzzy. Where there are specific requirements or prohibitions, these usually have been placed on the books as the result of an executive or legislative judgment that a situation or practice needed correction or regulation. We also operate under Executive orders which have the force of law, but which can be changed by the president without reference to Congress and the courts. These are a little more specific than the *U.S. Code*, but may not provide guidance in all cases. Executive orders issued by Presidents Ford, Carter and Reagan all specifically prohibit the use of assassination. This structure was established as the result of congressional investigations that uncovered efforts, albeit unsuccessful, to murder specific foreign political figures. Despite this guidance, questions continue to be raised in the press about CIA practices in this regard, and some observers do not see the presidential order as guidance which has universal applicability.

If laws and regulations do not provide adequate moral guidance, what can you fall back on? And what is customary and proper in intelligence operations is hard to codify and particularly hard to provide to new employees. We all have a personal sense of what is right and proper, but how do we evolve an institutional sense—what are the traditions within our profession, and how do these correspond with what this nation, through its citizens and their elected representatives, consider to be justifiable and moral options?

Here we find the crux of the dilemma. In an open democratic system of government, "We the People" govern, and each federal official is ultimately responsible to the people. But how can you keep the people adequately informed about sensitive intelligence operations? Even if they knew the details, they frequently would not comprehend the whys and wherefores of the conduct of clandestine operations. The principal question, therefore, is whether public sentiment can serve as an adequate judge of the ethics of our profession. We have tried to formalize this through the use of congressional oversight. This has provided for collective responsibility on the part of both the executive and legislative branches of our government, but recent press reports indicate that there remains considerable skepticism in public about the effectiveness of this system.

It is necessary at this time to outline some of the types of intelligence activities considered in this essay, so that we can discuss the ethical principles which apply to each of them. The first category involves clandestine intelligence collection operations which are meant to be secret. We are attempting to obtain information denied to us through normal means. In fact, other governments, especially in closed societies, use specific methods to prevent us from learning information they wish to restrict. We use various methods, including the use of human agents, and spies, whom we recruit to obtain the information using clandestine methods. This, by its very nature, requires a certain amount of deception. Our officers serving overseas need to have cover stories to protect their clandestine operations. Because every nation considers spying to be illegal and those who get caught are subject to severe penalties, cover stories are important not only for the safety of intelligence officers, but also to protect our agents and our very ability to conduct espionage. The deception is not intended to be malicious; it is used to hide the true identity and purpose of those involved in what we consider to be legitimate aspects of espionage. In moral terms, a certain amount of operational deception is proper if used to protect the clandestine operation and those involved in it. It is not proper if used to hide embarrassing outcomes from the American people.

There is clearly a requirement for a certain amount of deception in clandestine operations. At times we must make others believe that we are doing something that is plausibly innocent when in fact we are conducting secret operations. This is an extension of the principle of cover and provides the clandestine officer a means to open a door or peek through a window so that a secret operation can be undertaken. Clandestine operations to gather information inevitably involve human relationships as well. A recruitment is frequently made on the basis of personal friendship and mutual trust. Nevertheless, the intelligence officer must have some measure of control. Thus, these relationships may involve manipulation or deception. To what extent are the practices needed to maintain control "honorable?" Does this create a moral dilemma for the intelligence officer involved in such operations?

Clandestine operations are considered to be correct and morally justifiable as long as they are conducted on the basis that they are needed to protect the state. But they would not be morally justifiable if they violated the basic principles for which we stand and the institutional traditions of this intelligence service.

That is easily said, but how do we, as professional intelligence officers, know what is morally justifiable and what is not? Under what standard do we operate? Who sets the rules and how do we apply them in a given situation? It certainly encompasses more than the intelligence laws, and the ethics of this institution and profession do differ markedly from any other body of personal or professional ethics. (In fact, we come closer to those ethics which apply to the military profession than most intelligence officers recognize.)

In order to provide some kind of guideline, we have developed what we call the Chomeau-Rudolph proposal. It holds that:

—We follow the guidelines for duty, honor, and country.
—We upgrade these principles using "just war" theory as a systematic approach to ethical problems inherent in intelligence operations and analysis.

The goal of the Chomeau-Rudolph proposal is to increase the morally appropriate options available to professional intelligence officers.

Duty. Duty is the obligation not only to do the job, but within ethical norms. Therefore, one needs a knowledge of the moral principles and a facility developed through practice in applying them.

Honor. Honor emphasizes moral development to be as important as physical, intellectual, tradecraft and other criteria of professional competence.

Country. By country, we mean seeking to uphold the Constitution, but this should extend beyond the strictly legal underpinnings to cover other criteria of professional competence.

We have determined that the most sensible basis for justifying the use of intelligence operations corresponds with the general principles for the use of military power in the protection of the nation-state. Thus, we have turned to the Just War theory to provide a framework for establishing moral principles for intelligence. Making moral assessments on complex matters requires applying universal principles and making prudent judgments. The variables involved in these moral assessments include: (1) the type of logic involved, (2) the perceptions of the facts as they apply to the case at hand, and (3) the values of the judges.

The logic we have employed starts with the basic deontological principles favoring nonintervention, honesty, and trust in another country until such time that holding such values can cause more harm than good. In other words, the burden is put on the consequentialist who must argue a case for a departure from the absolute moral principles. A consequentialist may be justified in recommending a clandestine operation to counter the hostile actions of another country against us or the use of deception to protect U.S. interests or operations.

The accurate perception of facts, in a mass of noise and attempts on the parts of others to confuse us, is a critical part of our profession. Knowledge is our product. We endeavor to maintain analytical objectivity, for it is key to the integrity of our work. Analytical perceptions which have been distorted by policy preferences, political ideologies, and personal bias may obscure the facts. We must ever be cognizant of these pressures, and potential dilemmas created when policy skews analytical judgments.

Finally, the values of the judges—our policy-level consumers and the American public—become the true arbiter of the activities of the intelligence system. Frequently we must consider what projects will look like to the public when (not if) exposed. But people who are basically moral can reach quite different conclusions about what is right or wrong. In intelligence operations there is no truly objective right or wrong which is universally understood. We must attempt to operate within a scheme of ethical norms which is commonly understood and applicable to our profession. We believe that this scheme is contained in Just War theory.

The Just War principles have evolved over the centuries and are well understood to apply to the ethical standards to be followed by a nation at war. Since the major function of intelligence is to provide early and adequate warning of an attack by forces inimical to the nation, one can derive an extension of the Just War principles to intelligence. The CIA was formed in 1947 primarily to protect the United States against a growing Soviet threat and to ensure that we would suffer no more Pearl Harbors. Initial focus was almost exclusively on the USSR and its allies, but recent threats to this nation have taken so many other forms that we have come to use intelligence to provide timely and accurate information on a whole host of issues that affect the security of the U.S. and its people, including economic and agricultural problems overseas, as well as problems such as terrorism and narcotics.

To review briefly the *jus ad bellum* requirements:

—just cause—defend one's state, citizens, allies.
—just intent—restoration of peace, freedom.
—probability of success—can we pull it off?
—proportional objectives—counterintervention, preserve secrecy of operation.
—last resort—all options considered, exploited.
—ordered by competent authority—president, DCI, etc.

The *jus in bello* requirements are:

—discrimination—no assassination, invoke double effect principle.
—proportionality—cause limited damage, undertake "acceptable risk."

A reasonable explanation for intelligence capability is the argument of the consequentialist who remains true to the value of Duty, Country, and Honor but can justify a departure from the prohibition on the use of force.

The consequentialist is justified for arguing for a use of force given

that the superpower nature of the US places such an obligation on it that not acting in a certain situation could be more evil than acting. Policymakers as well as intelligence officers must consider the right thing to do in the context of the real, rather than the ideal or hoped for situation . . . and the price of neglect may be too high. In many instances the instrument of choice in the conduct of foreign affairs is the quiet and deniable use of intelligence resources instead of the more forceful and overt means, such as military force. But there are some serious considerations, including the ability of political leaders to develop a consensus that the non-war options are viable and acceptable. How does one integrate the wishes of the American people and to what extent should their intentions control the planning and execution of intelligence operations? If secrecy is an executive privilege in our society, how we do protect our secrets from other components of our own society? Some effort must be made to weigh the moral imperatives against the possibility of damage to the nation if secret operations are not used.

Staying for the moment within the rubric of clandestine intelligence collection, the principles outlined above suggest that you must seek information in which this government has a legitimate interest. Operations simply for their own sake are not justifiable. The officer seeking approval for a particular collection effort needs to have a specific goal in mind in order to gain approval. The CIA has an internal review mechanism to assure this is the case. The principle of "just means" is a little more murky, but there are well-understood professional standards included in what we call tradecraft, or the proper conduct of clandestine operations. These principles are taught to all clandestine service officers. An officer who departs from the norm or uses unethical means to gain information runs the risk of criticism, reprimand, and endangering future operations.

The principles of last resort and proportionality come together in the conduct of clandestine operations. Our officers understand that they should be working to collect only that type of information which cannot be collected overtly by State Department officers, or through clandestine technical means; then the case officer should question whether the use of an agent is proper. Sometimes the agent will be asked to provide reporting in order to verify or amplify data from other sources, but that would still meet the criteria of last resort and proportionality.

The last criterion, likelihood of success, is one of the most troublesome. Sometimes the information desired is so valuable that extremely high risks and costs in an attempt to gain it are justifiable. In every operation the key questions to be asked are how much risk can be accepted, what is the potential payoff, and what penalties would have to be paid if the operation failed. As with the rest of clandestine operations, these principles are taught in training programs for clandestine service officers and are part of the review process undertaken before CIA Headquarters approval is given.

Let us review a few illustrations of the types of dilemmas faced by clandestine officers. All would agree that it is wrong for government officials to accept a bribe. Is it wrong for an intelligence officer to give a bribe in the course of operations to accomplish the task? There are many areas of the world where bribery is an accepted norm. Another interesting situation might involve a cover story that is starting to unravel. The basic principle in the use of cover is deniability. Should an officer deny association with intelligence—that is, lie—to maintain cover? Intelligence officers are taught to maintain cover even if taken prisoner and there is ample evidence about the activity in question. Is it a lie and immoral to persist in a cover story at that time? A good example is the U-2 incident in which Francis Gary Powers was shot down over the Soviet Union. His cover story was that he was on a weather reconnaissance flight and had gotten lost. President Eisenhower stuck with the cover story despite clear evidence that, first, Powers was alive and, second, that the Soviets had recovered part of the aircraft. When Khrushchev paraded the evidence out in front of Soviet television cameras, however, deniability was gone. At that point, President Eisenhower came forward and assumed complete responsibility for the operation. This was proper, for to continue in the denial was no longer justifiable in an attempt to protect sources and methods. They had been totally compromised. To continue to deny would be to lie without purpose or effect.

A totally different set of problems arises in the area of intelligence analysis. These problems may result in part from the separation between operations and analysis. While there is good communication between the officers involved in both activities, the functions are quite distinct, and because of compartmentation—or "need-to-know"—analysts and operations officers carry out their tasks in what might seem to be two different cultures. Nevertheless, they must understand their collective responsibility to the system as a whole. One of the points we attempt to inculcate in training is that *all* agency officers are collectively responsible for whatever the CIA does. An analyst cannot distance himself or herself from operations and say "that is not part of my business and I don't know what is really going on in the clandestine side of the agency anyhow."

In the business of intelligence analysis, principles of business ethics may provide better guidelines than the "just war principles" which we have applied to clandestine operations. The CIA analytical function was set up to provide to the DCI and to the White House a truly independent group of country and technical experts who could determine the threats to the U.S. as they saw them. Intelligence analysts must not get involved in the formulation and implementation of policy, nor can they construct their analysis so as to favor one particular policy position over another. This means that the CIA analyst must walk a very fine line in order to provide information which is both objective and policy or program relevant without taking sides in the internal fights within the administration which frequently evolve over these issues. In addition to providing intelligence to the executive branch, CIA also provides intelligence analysis to the Congress. In the U.S. system, that inevitably means that the agency will be providing information to a legislative body that may seek to overturn, stop, or alter the policies of the executive. That raises the question of "For whom are we really working?" Former DCI William Colby, just prior to his testimony before a Senate committee, responded to that question by saying that our obligation is to the truth.

All analysts have personal opinions and biases. It is hard to write a truly objective article which does not in some way reflect how the analyst feels about the issue. We used to say, when training analysts, "are you starting with the premise that the glass is half-full or half-empty?" If an analyst believes that the administration is off on the wrong track, is it proper to attempt to steer or change policy through analysis? Some analysts believe that they should try to change the views of policymakers through their analysis—not understanding that high-level policy decisions are based on many other factors than just the "objective" facts and interpretations provided by intelligence specialists.

The most serious ethical problem faced by intelligence analysts is the attempt by others to politicize their product. The CIA by and large has been able to stand back from policy and program squabbles, but it is very possible to state what is considered to be a nonpolitical view and discover that the analyst has lined up on the side of one of the principal policymakers and has perhaps alienated others. Sometimes, then, what is perceived as politicization is only an association of our analysis with a specific policy position. Most intelligence analysts jealously guard their position as guardians of the truth and resist strenuously any attempts to co-opt them. Sometimes, however, we go so far in an attempt to maintain our independence and objectivity that we find ourselves taking a line of reasoning which argues a position which is in opposition to a policy which has been espoused by the administration.

There are enough checks and balances built into the system so that the view of any one analyst does not get out until it has been reviewed and coordinated with all the other analysts who have an interest in the subject. There is also a very cumbersome, but necessary, mechanism for editorial and managerial review of papers before they are published. If an individual analyst believes that he or she is not being adequately heard on a key issue or that his or her analysis has been politicized, there are several avenues of appeal. There have been a few analysts who have resigned in protest and taken their case to the American people (as did Sam Adams over the differences in the counts of enemy forces in Vietnam), but these cases are quite rare.

Covert action, which can be quite controversial, is the type of intelligence issue most frequently discussed in the media. It accounts for only a small fraction of CIA's overall effort and does not relate either to the collection of secret information or the production of intelligence analysis. It does provide a covert means to the administration for the execution of U.S. policy overseas. That the CIA is the executive agent for most covert activity on behalf of the U.S. Government is almost an accident of history. When the national security apparatus (including the National Security Council, the Department of Defense and the Central Intelligence Agency) was being created in 1947, the logical place to put the responsibility for covert action was in the CIA. These kinds of operations had been performed well by the OSS in World War II. It seemed to make sense to continue to use those methods as the Cold War began in earnest; and although we can not brag about our successes, covert action has made a positive impact in many instances.

The major feature of covert action is that it is deniable, i.e., that the hand of the U.S. Government is hidden and deniable. It is designed, in part, to head off nasty situations overseas which could harm the United States and its interests and secretly to favor those who are most likely to support us. Many of the recipients of U.S. covert assistance would be seriously compromised should the fact of the covert action be known. For this reason, it is necessary to take extraordinary measures to protect these relationships. Unfortunately, in recent years thanks to investigative work on the part of some journalists and because of leaks of sensitive information, the details of many of these covert activities have been compromised. Such revelations force the intelligence and policy communities into even greater secrecy and can set up great pressures on those charged with the protection of intelligence sources and methods. This creates a dilemma which has been faced by every DCI since Richard Helms. The DCI must balance the need to protect the viability of clandestine assets against the obligation to keep both the Executive and the Congress informed about intelligence operations.

There are no clear principles which apply in the use of clandestine or covert action. Each case must be judged on its own merits. There is once again implied in "just war" theory a basis for the right of one government to interfere in the affairs of another, so long as the principles of just cause, just means, proportionality, etc., prevail. It is where they are exceeded or ignored that we run the risk of conducting a covert operation which violates both the principles of the agency and the nation.

The major moral principle we would set for the conduct of covert action is that it should be the sort of thing that would be acceptable to the American people, if its details were revealed—remember what we said earlier about "We the People." The final judge in these matters appears to be American public opinion as reported in our public media and expressed through our elected representatives. The problem is that we are not dealing with an informed public in most instances relating to espionage and covert actions. Does the public appear to trust either officials of the administration or their elected representatives to do what is right and proper? Just mention the name CIA in some circles in this country and you conjure visions of agents working the back alleys of the world doing things that Americans would not approve of. To make our system of checks and balances work, someone must do a more effective job explaining the why of what we are doing without revealing any of the secret specifics. In that sense, the intelligence system is dependent on the White House to explain its use of intelligence resources within the bounds of secrecy, and it is also dependent on the Congress which must learn not only what is going on, but also keep in mind what the American people would think about such operations.

If the American people are truly the final arbiters of policy in this country, and of what is ethical and moral, they need to have enough of an understanding of what is at stake to make informed judgments on these matters.

So what ethical construct do we have and how do we teach it in the classroom? First, it is patently clear that despite the problems of defining, in a universal sense, what is ethical, the CIA needs to have a commitment to teaching ethics to its employees. The nature of our work is such that it is not sufficient merely to depend upon hiring the right people. Loyalty to the agency as well as an understanding of what is appropriate in various situations can be taught in the classroom and handed down from one generation of intelligence officers to the next. Each CIA employee comes to us with a strong personal set of moral values. We are very careful to screen for these and to hire "honorable men." In our training and orientation programs, we strive to inform our officers of laws and regulations relating to our profession as well as to instill in them some of the ethos of the CIA and our traditions. Old hands usually take the newer officers under their wings and help them develop an understanding of the sensitive nature of our work and some of the principles which govern our behavior. In training classes, we frequently resort to case studies and a discussion of the pros and cons of some of the more sticky operations. It is necessary that every CIA officer has an adequate understanding of what the other components are doing—without revealing even to other CIA employees the details of the more sensitive operations. Nevertheless, the bottom line is that there is no code, no universally understood set of principles. In our work, the end does not justify the means, but it frequently charts the course which must be taken. It is up to the professional intelligence officer to choose the right and proper course of action to obtain the proper results. Just War principles can help, but the final judge does appear to be what the American people and their elected representative would hold to be necessary and proper.

PART III

TRAINING
FOR ETHICAL BEHAVIOR
IN THE ARMED FORCES

HOW SHALL WE INCORPORATE ETHICS INSTRUCTION AT ALL LEVELS?

DANIEL CALLAHAN
The Hastings Center

Dr. Callahan acknowledges the indifference and outright resistance that often affect the teaching of professional ethics. He urges clear, limited goals for ethics courses, and he offers suggestions for the conduct of these courses.

The question I want to address is how we are to situate, understand, and pursue the effective teaching of professional ethics.

One immediate reaction to proposals to teach professional ethics or efforts to improve already existing teaching, is to become quite restless with the "theoretical" issues. There is a great tendency to feel that they need to be put aside because they are often endless and deep—one needs simply to get down to the practical issues: how do you teach the subject, what kind of material to use, and so on.

My own strong conviction is that the theoretical issues must be dealt with at all times, and cannot be pushed to the background. There surely are practical problems in the teaching of ethics, but a greater number of them in both obvious and subtle ways continue to turn on the very nature of ethics itself. Ethics is, obviously enough, a subject with a long human history, and a history marked by a great deal of dispute and controversy. In his dialogue the "Meno," Plato has Meno ask Socrates, at the very opening, "Can virtue be taught?" As is typical of the dialogues, Socrates gives no definitive answer to that question, and it is one that has remained with us ever since.

We argue about ethics because it is so fundamental, and because how we ought to live our lives is a very difficult problem. Moreover, when one talks about the teaching of ethics in particular fields, whether in elementary schools, in colleges, in professional schools, in military commands, or anywhere else, there will be disputes about that as well. Most of those disputes are intimately involved with questions about what ethics itself is. The teaching of ethics in the professions, then, must always have some relationship to those long-standing arguments and disputes, and though they are theoretical, and difficult, they are part of what we must grapple with. We cannot really do a good job with the practical issues unless we are alert to some of the inherent difficulties of the subject matter itself.

The teaching of professional ethics also has to combat a great deal of indifference, or sometimes outright hostility, to the subject matter itself. Professionals are often resistant to the teaching of ethics. Sometimes the resistance stems from the rather widespread belief that it is an inherently soft and mushy topic. A common enough belief in our society, at least among many, is that ethics is nothing but a matter of taste and preference or perhaps the private religious values of people. Therefore, there is nothing one can teach in any rational way, and therefore there is really no subject matter than can effectively be taught.

Another objection, less often stated but I believe always present, is that the very subject itself is a disturbing and controversial one, and one does best to avoid it. There is no doubt that the teaching of ethics can be disturbing. If it is well done, it forces a confrontation with our basic professional goals; it makes us look at our daily practices; and it makes us ask what it is after all we are living for, working for, and leading our professional lives for. A lot of people do not want to confront those questions. They might not like what they find, and they know it.

Still another objection is that too much concern about ethics can be incompatible with competence. It is sometimes felt that, as professionals, people need to be trained in various technical and specialized skills, and trained also to act rapidly and decisively. It is sometimes thought that ethics simply introduces a great deal of muddle, confusion, and indecision into thinking, and therefore ethics will get in the way of acting in a professionally competent fashion.

It is important to be aware of objections of every kind, even if they are not stated. I think it reasonable to assume that there is uncertainty, suspicion, and skepticism about the subject of professional ethics.

I believe, however, that ethics can be effectively taught and communicated if one's goals are clear and reasonably limited. The subject is not inherently soft and mushy, though it can certainly be treated that way, and, if poorly handled, can convey to people the notion that there are no clear answers about anything. That is simply false.

The most important thing, however, in even thinking about the teaching of ethics is to clarify the goals. In our work on the teaching of professional ethics, The Hastings Center developed some very general goals, of a kind we think is appropriate in a professional setting. There is, first of all, the need to alert people to the very existence of ethical problems. A great number of people are not very sensitive about that, and it is important to try to instill into them the ability to spot an ethical issue, to be sensitive to its nuances, and to have some sense of how to proceed with it. A second goal is closely related to that: the training of people to be able to analyze the ethical problems once they encounter them. Ethics is something people can think about in ways that are better or worse, and a great part of the teaching of ethics is simply to help people to clarify their thinking, to push forward in a relentless fashion with some of the problems and attempt to reach some kind of conclusions. A third and critical ingredient is that of stimulating a sense of personal obligation. Ethics can be talked about in an abstract impersonal way, implying that it is not anybody's personal business at all. But the teaching of ethics will get nowhere or will be utterly meaningless unless the instructor, or the program, is attempting always to get people to take it seriously, to feel that they have a personal obligation to behave well, to think hard about their ethical life, and to consider carefully the ethical implications of their behavior for their professional activities. Ethics, in short, is inherently a practical and applied discipline, one meant to stimulate people to behave as well as they can.

The fourth and final goal we developed is that of both tolerating and resisting the ambiguity of ethics. Ethics often puts people off because it seems that progress cannot be made with the issues, that the controversies are too extensive. On the contrary, people need to be alerted to the fact there is a great deal of ambiguity and uncertainty in making ethical decisions, and that one has to develop a certain toleration for that uncertainty. At the same time, it is important to underscore the fact that progress can be made with the problems and that the uncertainty can often be reduced. Hence, the kind of paradoxical combination of toleration of and resistance to uncertainty must be a fundamental part of the teaching of ethics.

Once one has some general goals in mind, then one can better take account of some of the criticisms and objections that I mentioned above. Ethics is and should be a disturbing subject. If it is pursued well and responsibly, people should be led to ask about their basic purposes, as individual human beings and as military officers. The ethics of a profession, I believe, always follows the goals and purposes of a profession. Ethics, to put the matter another way, is not something one simply adds on the professional goals and purposes but is very fundamental to their achievement. Ethics is often disturbing because it forces people to ask what it is they are all about and what goals they are seeking as individual people and as professionals. Many people don't want to think about that, but that is one of the primary purposes in the teaching of ethics.

The objection that ethics may perhaps make people, particularly military officers, less competent, seems to me just plain wrong. Good ethical thinking is nothing more than responsible analysis, self-examination, and a recognition that ethics is a fundamental part of making technical and professional decisions. People cannot, of course, read Aristotle in the middle of a battle, or sit down and ponder very difficult moral dilemmas in the midst of a crisis. But they can think about those issues before, much as they can with all other fields in military or other forms of professional life. What one does with the teaching of ethics is to try to get people to think in advance, to be prepared for crises and hard decisions when they arise. The problem in assuming that ethics and competence are working against each other is the failure to recognize that one cannot be a competent professional unless one is a moral and responsible professional. Immoral behavior may, so to speak, work for a time. But the history of our institutions, including the history of warfare itself, indicates that bad moral behavior usually turns back upon itself; it is usually harmful to oneself and one's interests. Competence and ethics go fundamentally together.

In the same vein, it is sometimes said that the "real world" is resistant to ethics. That is true sometimes, but the real world is not something that is utterly fixed. One of the purposes of teaching ethics is to convey to individuals, and to institutions, that the real world can be changed, that it is malleable, that it is subject to the values people bring to bear on it. The notion that there is some nasty real world out there, ever against some pure and clean ethical world, seems to me false. The real world is shot through with values, some good and some bad, and that world can be changed, just as the individuals who inhabit the world can also be changed.

In short, I think one has to fight very hard against the notion of any incompatibility between ethics and competence. On the contrary, the main message in the teaching of ethics has to be that the two are one and the same; there is no such thing as a technical decision that does not have its ethical implications and will not be influenced by the moral considerations of those who have to make decisions, give commands, or take action.

What can one hope to reasonably accomplish with the teaching of ethics? It is important to get straight on this question, since many people expect the teaching of ethics to accomplish much more than it possibly can, and one simply opens the way for a great deal of disappointment if there is not some general understanding about what is possible and what is not possible.

It is certainly possible to signal the existence of moral issues. That ought at least to be a minimal goal, and one that can be accomplished. One needs to find ways to quickly and readily identify the moral problems that people in the military will encounter, and to label them as ethical where that is appropriate and justified. Even if people don't take the whole subject seriously, they will at least know that there are ethical problems out there. I think that one next has to show that those problems are closely related to the competent discharge of one's duties. Here we go back to the question of the relationship between ethics and competence, and I think one has to do everything possible to show that the two are closely related.

I think it is no less a basic goal to give people, whether officers or enlisted men, some sense of why ethical problems arise. Ethical problems do not arise out of a vacuum: they are usually the result of certain situations or institutional arrangements or other structural elements. The fundamental goal of anyone who tries to be ethical should be to avoid terrible ethical dilemmas in the first place. Frequently, ethical dilemmas are a result of bad institutional arrangements. The people in those institutions should not even have such problems; that is, they should not have the problems if things were properly ordered and managed. In any case, it is important to give people some sense of why ethical problems arise, and what their institutional and social setting is.

I think it is perfectly feasible to show that thinking about ethics can be helpful, productive, and interesting. It is a great mistake in teaching ethics to begin with the worst possible dilemma one can think of. That simply discourages people, and makes them depressed about the whole subject. Moreover, all of the moral life does not consist of dealing with utterly impossible dilemmas but usually with simpler situations. I think the teaching of ethics should best begin with rather simple issues and problems, where some agreement can quickly be reached, and then move on to the harder ones. Pick cases that touch on people's lives and experiences, make them as interesting as possible, and do everything to stimulate their imaginations.

I think it is very important to use consultation heavily and extensively. Ethics is the kind of subject best handled by discussion, rather than by the didactic lecture. I say this for a very simple reason: the teaching of ethics is as much a process as a result, that is, a process of getting people to think well and responsibly about their moral lives and the moral dilemmas they will encounter. The result is, so to speak, the very process of the thinking itself. The more involvement one can get in even identifying the problems, and in talking out the problems, the faster one will move toward effective teaching.

I think it is important also to be prepared to move back and forth between some of the theoretical questions and some of the practical questions. The old issue of "Why should I be moral?"—a question that is close to 2,500 years old—will continue to arise as much now as it did for earlier generations. You have to be prepared to cope with that very theoretical and very difficult question. Moreover, one has to be prepared to deal with the questions of where we get our moral rules? how do you justify moral obligations? how do you develop notions of what are appropriate virtues for people? The justification of all such things requires some kind of theoretical foundation. It is a mistake to try to dodge those questions, even if one does not feel one can handle them adequately. No one can handle them adequately, since they are very hard and very old, but it is the process of seriously trying to do so that is often most convincing, and the most that any of us can do in any event. The final thing I would say is that there are really no hard and fast ways for effectively teaching ethics. We have to each find that method that works best for ourselves and that enables us to convey the importance of the subject— the need for personal character—and the possibility of effectively combining professional competence and moral behavior. I think one ought constantly to experiment with teaching methods and techniques. Don't be rigidly fixed on what is likely to be more or less effective. The important thing is to steadily pursue the centrality of morality in the professional life, to try to understand that professional life, and to know the way in which moral problems present themselves to individuals as they carry out their professional activities. A seriousness of purpose is the most important ingredient in good teaching.

TEACHING THE LAW
OF WAR

W. HAYS PARKS
Colonel, Marine Corps Reserve

Colonel Parks, a Special Assistant for Law of War Matters in the Office of The Judge Advocate General of the Army, describes origins of the law of war and outlines current programs for teaching the law of war in the Marine Corps and the Army. He also provides a number of lessons that emerged from efforts to develop successful instruction in the law of war.

The law of war as we know it today probably had its origins in the post-World War II trials of German and Japanese war criminals. While substantial elements of the modern law of war existed prior to World War II, the massive suffering of total war provided the impetus for clarification and codification of the law. The war crimes trials at Nuremberg, Tokyo, and other sites established clearly the individual criminal responsibility of military men who violate the law of war. The four 1949 Geneva Conventions for the Protection of War Victims expanded the codified law of war beyond protection just for wounded and captured soldiers to military personnel wounded or ship-wrecked at sea, and to certain segments of the civilian population.[1]

Ethics, morality, and the law often are described as strange bedfellows, perhaps incongruous if not contradictory; some also suggest that "law of war" is a contradiction in terms. I disagree with both propositions.

Nuremberg was based on ethical standards transposed to positive legal norms; the tribunals frequently used "moral," "ethical," and "legal" interchangeably although there are distinctions. The law of war is the vehicle by which nations have ethical concepts and apply them in concrete terms in the most demanding environment—mortal combat. Much of the law of war is based on the Just War tradition. Some parts remain elusive of definition or codification, while other parts have been expressly rejected. Thus there remains no agreed international definition for the concept of proportionality, while the four 1949 Geneva Conventions require application of their terms regardless of the justness of one's cause.[2]

The law of war reflects an attempt by nations to establish certain minimum standards of conduct by parties to armed conflict that will ameliorate the suffering of the innocent. As with all law, it is highly dependent on good faith by all concerned; at its best, it will not prevent all suffering. As Clausewitz warned, there is no way that war can be made "nice."[3] We have learned at considerable expense that when a nation endeavors to make war nice, or accepts limitations on the use of force beyond those required by law of war treaties, it does so at its peril. A less-moral nation will take advantage of its opponent's constraint, often to the detriment of the civilian population in the battle zone (as well as the military of the nation fighting with restraint). We were made painfully aware of this in the Vietnam war.[4] At the same time, failure to have a viable law of war program can be seen as a direct cause of the My Lai massacre.[5]

After the Vietnam war, the U.S. military revised its law of war program. A Department of Defense directive was promulgated, which provides that each individual will receive law of war training "commensurate with his or her duties and responsibilities."[6] This program is based on our treaty obligations and the constitutional premise that these treaties are part of the law of the land.[7] Upon entering the armed forces, each member of the United States military takes an oath to discharge his or her duties in accordance with the laws of the United States, including the law of war.

But no program can survive simply because "it's the law," and the Vietnam-era law of war programs suffered demonstrably because they endeavored to stand solely on the basis that certain conduct was expected on the battlefield "because the law says so." In 1968, the chief of staff of the Army wrote to the commander of the Military Assistance Command, Vietnam (MACV), noting his displeasure regarding recurring reports of mistreatment of prisoners of war. In response, the deputy commander, MACV, suggested that one reason was that judge-advocate-taught instruction in the law of war "has tended to be abstract and academic, rather than concrete and practical."[8]

Today's law of war programs emphasize the military and political reasons for respect for the law of war. Four basic assumptions form the foundation for the U.S. military program:

—Discipline in combat is essential.

—Violations of the law of war detract from a commander's accomplishment of his mission.

—Violations of the law of war frequently lead to a loss of public support (domestic and international) for the war effort.

—Violations of the law of war may arouse an enemy to greater resistance, leading to increased friendly casualties.

Similarly, the law of war is viewed as one of a number of control measures used by the battlefield commander to assist him in the efficient employment of his forces.[9] In comparing the definition of the law of war concept of military necessity, which authorizes "such destruction, and only such destruction, as is necessary, relevant, and proportionate to the prompt realization of legitimate military objectives," to a definition of the principle of war of economy of force, their common goal is clear: the efficient, discriminate use of force against legitimate targets. Each also coincides with the less-specific concepts of Just War and/or contemporary military ethics.[10]

Each military service has developed its law of war training program in accordance with its mission, and the realities of training time, of which there is never enough for the myriad demands upon a unit's or individual's time. The previously stated DOD standard ("commensurate with . . . duties and responsibilities") is one of relevancy. A sailor "shoveling steam" in the engine room of a ship needs to know far less than his battalion commander; a division or wing commander can look to his special staff (including his staff judge advocate) for expertise on law of war matters. In the competition for training time, law of war training is not keyed to nice to know, but to need to know in order to meet the DOD standard.

The Marine Corps Law of War Program establishes three levels of training:

Level A. The minimum level of understanding of the law of war required of all Marines principally to be received during accession training.

Level B. The levels of understanding necessary for personnel whose military specialty or assignment involves tactical planning or direct confrontation with the enemy, commensurate with their grade and responsibility.

Level C. The level of understanding necessary for judge advocates whose military assignment entails advisory responsibility to tactical commands.

At the lowest level, every individual entering the Marine Corps (enlisted and officer) receives two hours of instruction instilling in him or her nine basic principles:[11]

1. Marines fight only enemy combatants.
2. Marines do not harm enemy soldiers who surrender. Disarm them and turn them over to your superior.
3. Marines do not kill or torture prisoners.
4. Marines collect and care for the wounded, whether friend or foe.
5. Marines do not attack medical personnel, facilities, or equipment.
6. Marines destroy no more than the mission requires.
7. Marines treat all civilians humanely.
8. Marines do not steal. Marines respect private property

and possessions.
9. Marines should do their best to prevent violation of the law of war. Report all violations of the law of war to your superior.

There are sound military reasons behind each of these principles in addition to any moral or legal obligation and, like it or not, there is greater likelihood for respect for these principles if they are explained in military terms rather than solely from a moral or legal standpoint. For example, in instructing the individual Marine not to kill or torture prisoners of war, recognition of their intelligence potential carries greater weight than moral or legal values, which often are viewed as abstract and of questionable relevancy in the heat of battle. (It must be emphasized that tactical rationale is being used to support legal principles; Marines are taught that these nine principles are absolute and may not be waived when convenient.) Similarly, a lack of humane treatment may induce an enemy to fight to the death rather than surrender, thereby leading to increased friendly casualties. The instruction is candid, however, in admitting that humane treatment of enemy prisoners of war will not guarantee equal treatment for our captured servicemen, as we learned in World War II, Korea, and Vietnam, but it is emphasized that inhumane treatment will assuredly lead to equivalent actions by the enemy.[12]

Likewise, the admonition to "treat all civilians humanely" recognizes the need for a disciplined military force on the battlefield; a crime against a civilian on the battlefield is as much (and perhaps more) a detriment to unit discipline and integrity as one committed in Fayetteville, North Carolina, or

Oceanside, California, by a member of the military.[13] Mistreatment can alienate the civilian population. Abuses have a negative effect on public opinion, as evidenced by public reaction to the My Lai massacre.[14] But the instruction is given a common sense perspective in that it is acknowledged that civilians assume a certain degree of risk if they remain on the battlefield or in proximity to legitimate military targets, or participate in activities that directly support the war effort of the enemy.

To reach personnel at intermediate levels, law of war instruction is provided at the Staff Noncommissioned Officers Academy, Amphibious Warfare School, Communications Officer School, and Command and Staff College. Special courses also are offered. The Marine Corps Law of War course is a five-day course taught four to five times annually worldwide to company and field grade offices; the "mix" sought in each course is one-third each of judge advocates, ground officers (primarily combat arms), and aviators (fixed and rotary-wing). Its emphasis is on the practical rather than theoretical. Three days are spent on "Geneva" law relating to the protection of war victims, including prosecution of violations thereof; one day is devoted to "Hague" law, relating to means and methods of warfare; and final day classes address the law affecting peacetime military operations (including *jus ad bellum*) and the law relating to low-intensity conflict, including counterterrorism. In addition to Marine attendees, there have been students from the other U.S. services, Canada, the American National Red Cross, the League of Red Cross and Red Crescent Societies, and the International Committee of the Red Cross

(ICRC). A member of the ICRC addresses each class on the role of the ICRC in peacetime and armed conflict.

The Marine Corps Law of War course has been very successful. The key to its success lies in the knowledge of its instructors—all reservists, many with command experience in combat—of the law of war and the business of the client; the subject cannot be taught in the abstract. There are several manifestations of the success of the course. It comes first through applications to attend, which vastly exceed available billets; such is the reputation the course enjoys within the Marine Corps and the other military services. Student reaction also is significant. On the first day, even though they have applied to take the course, the members of the class generally are reserved as the students get to know one another and are exposed to the law of war in greater depth than previously. On the second and third days, lectures are interspersed with seminars in which students must address contemporary, "real world" problems; the officers warm to the subject, becoming more animated in their discussion and support for the law of war as wholly consistent with their doctrine, tactics, experience, common sense, and individual moral underpinnings. By the end of the course (despite an examination), they are avid enthusiasts for the law of war. One regimental commander described the course as the "best taught and most important course" he had attended in his entire career. A final manifestation of success was the recent award of a Meritorious Unit Citation by the Secretary of the Navy to the Marine Corps Reserve unit responsible for conduct of the course.[15]

Other courses are offered by the other services. For example, while continuing to utilize the Marine Corps Law of War course, the Navy offered its first law of war course at the Naval Justice School in Newport, Rhode Island, in 1985. Also, selected members of the U.S. military annually attend the twelve-day law of war course taught by the International Institute of Humanitarian Law in San Remo, Italy.

At a higher level, since 1982 the Army Judge Advocate General has sponsored annually a Military Operations and Law Symposium. This symposium is attended by active duty personnel by invitation only. Invitees are senior operations planners for major U.S. commands worldwide and their staff judge advocates.[16] There also is limited allied participation. Representatives from the United Kingdom, Canada, Australia, and New Zealand attended the 1984 symposium, for example, and spent the week preceding the symposium discussing common law of war issues.

The purpose of the symposium is to bring together key personnel to discuss contemporary operational-legal issues in a classified environment. Previous topics have included rules of engagement, navigation and overflight rights, peacekeeping operations, the 1981 Gulf of Sidra incident, the 1982 Falklands War (a British presentation), the 1983 Grenada rescue operation; and operations against Libya in 1986. In an effort to keep the law abreast of technology, subjects such as beyond-visual-range targeting and over-the-horizon targeting—both tied to the moral/level concept of discrimination—also have been addressed. Each symposium has been an unqualified success.

Other blocks of instruction are tailored to the audience. A class on "Medical Personnel and the Law of War" is given for the Uniformed Services University for the Health Sciences (in Bethesda) and for prospective commanding officers of Naval medical facilities (also at Bethesda) and the U.S. Army Academy of the Health Sciences Advanced Combat Casualty Care Course (Fort Sam Houston). Targeting and the law of war is taught at the Air Command and Staff College (Maxwell Air Force Base) and the Air Force Target Intelligence Course (Lowry Air Force Base). "The Law Affecting Special Operations" is a classified presentation given special operations personnel who attend the Joint Special Operations Planning Workshop at the U.S. Air Force Special Operations School (Hurlburt Field). Less specialized but tailored blocks are offered at other service schools, such as the Army War College, Armed Forces Staff College, and the U.S. Navy Chaplain's School. This list is not all-inclusive but is merely representative of the wide variety of courses in which the law of war instruction offered within the U.S. military is at least double that of any other nation.

One reason for the breadth and depth of U.S. law of war instruction is that we are a nation dedicated to the rule of law. Another is to make the future commander aware of the complexities of today's law while advising him of his responsibilities under that law. Recognizing the importance of compliance with the law of war in the conduct of U.S. military operations, the Joint Chiefs of Staff in 1979 promulgated a requirement that all operations plans, contingency plans, and rules of engagement undergo a legal review as part of the JCS operational review process. That directive was expanded and repromulgated in 1983, in part, as follows:[17]

Conduct of Operations. Legal advisors should be immediately available to provide advice concerning law of war compliance during joint and combined operations. Such advice on law of war compliance shall be provided in the context of the broader relationships of international and U.S. and allied domestic law to military operations and, among other matters, shall address not only legal restraints upon operations but also legal rights to employ force.

Review of Joint Documents. All plans, rules of engagement, policies and directives shall be consistent with the DOD Law of War Program, domestic and international law, and shall include, as necessary, provisions for (1) the conduct of military operations and exercises in accordance with laws affecting such operations, including the law of war violations, whether committed by or against U.S. or allied military or civilians or their property. Such joint documents should be reviewed by the joint command legal advisor at each state of preparation.

The "proof of the pudding," however, does not rest solely on formal instruction and review of plans. Because of the competition for training time, as well as the need for realistic, hands-on training, an increasing number of law of war problems are being built into field (and fleet) exercises at all levels. For example, the greatest reinforcement for classroom instruction on the handling of a prisoner of war has proved to be actual handling and processing of an "enemy" prisoner of war from the point of capture to turnover to appropriate authority. Other reinforcement measures have been instituted. The Judge Advocate General of the Army includes law of war issues as part of the special interest items for Article 6, UCMJ, inspections; the Air Force includes law of war questions in operational readiness inspections; while the Center for Naval War Gaming at the Naval War College routinely incorporates law of war issues into its war games. These approaches have proved far more effective than forcing troops into a classroom to watch the same, outdated movie periodically, as previously was the case, while reaching all levels of command.

This approach to law of war training paid dividends during the planning of operations against Libya, both in the early freedom-of-navigation exercises and the subsequent airstrikes against terrorist-related targets. Law of war experts at the USEUCOM, service, and JCS level assisted mission planners with promulgation of rules of engagement, selection of targets, and anticipation and consideration of other possible law of war issues. A close, working relationship was one of the many factors that led to successful conclusion of each mission.[18]

Conclusion. I have endeavored to summarize current law of war training efforts within the U.S. military to explain one approach that is being taken in one aspect of ethics instruction. I do not wish to suggest that current service programs are perfect. There are shortfalls, and it is a continuous effort to identify and correct them. In the review of U.S. operations in Grenada, it was discovered that one unit had conducted no law of war training in the year preceding that rescue operation. That no offenses occurred is testimony to the quality of the leadership within the unit and to the consistency of the law of war with common sense and military doctrine. But it reminded us that a program is dependent on individuals and their interest in or support for the law of war. It has served as an impetus for review of law of war training to establish methods for ensuring that law of war training is conducted within units. Other improvements will be made where needed.

Law of war training has made great strides in all of the services over the past decade. Whereas previously the subject was received with passive resistance or in some cases outright skepticism, today it is greeted with active interest if not vigorous enthusiasm—provided it is presented properly. I close by offering some lessons learned from developing these law of war programs.

1. *Have faith in the student.* The men and women of today's military are intelligent, dedicated professionals, with a greater sense for what is moral or legal than we give them credit for having. They don't believe in Rambo any more than they believe in Jane Fonda. The historical emphasis of this nation on the citizen-soldier means that our military is a cross-section of our society with its Judeo-Christian heritage. More often than not we are preaching to the choir.

2. *Be positive in your instruction.* Past law of war instruction has suffered many sins, not the least of which was a heavy dose of negativism; instructors tended to emphasize that which was prohibited, and were reluctant to acknowledge that anything was permitted. In fact, the law of war permits more than it prohibits, and instruction today emphasizes rights as well as responsibilities.

3. *Ascertain what is relevant to your audience, and teach in the vocabulary of the audience.* Several years ago I attended a law of war conference at the Naval War College; in those days the entire student body of the college sat in the large auditorium for three days while law of war experts engaged in a highly esoteric "lovefest" in which they praised one another while talking about subjects of interest only to themselves and of relevance to no one. One particular scholar read a paper on the various ways in which you classify an individual captured in battle a prisoner of war that was totally irrelevant to the modern battlefield.

Like ethics, the law of war can be a very esoteric subject. But it also involves common sense, and instruction offered in terms of the student's work and in the vocabulary of his profession will go far towards convincing him or her of the importance of our subjects to his or her work.

4. *Pose the right questions.* One of the most controversial law of war scenarios with which to deal concerns a four-man reconnaissance team being pursued by enemy forces deep in hostile territory that stumbles upon an enemy soldier clearly within minutes of death from a fatal wound. If the team leaves the soldier alone, he may be found by its pursuers before he dies, endangering their survival. If the soldiers stay with the soldier until he dies from his wound, they probably will be detected. Yet to hasten his inevitable death through another violent act would constitute a violation of the law of war.

The odds against this situation occurring to any particular individual are greater than the national debt. Yet some law of war instructors insisted on self-destruction by starting with this scenario, thereby losing the students for the balance of their presentation.

My point is that there are hypothetical questions with answers, and others that can be debated until the cows come home without reaching an acceptable answer. Gaining credibility for your subject is achieved by going from easy to difficult though, of course, you must be prepared to address the tough questions when they are raised. Similarly, while we should encourage reasoning, thinking, and questioning, we should not select an approach that does little more than cast doubt. Many students enter a classroom environment with a suspicion that many of the things they might be asked to do are illegal or immoral—but knowing that they will do them anyway. The myths regarding prohibited acts abound in the realm of the law of war. By correcting those myths and reassuring students that their doctrine and tactics are in accordance with the law of war, and explaining to them the consistency of the law of war with these things, the students gain confidence in what they are doing—and understand better the need for the prohibitions that do exist.

5. *Understand history.* Neither ethics nor the law of war can be taught in a vacuum. A keen sense of history is essential to teaching ethical or legal concepts. Otherwise these concepts appear to stand in stark contrast with what students believe is history. For example, frequently I am asked to reconcile the law of war with the strategic air offensive against Germany or, more specifically, the bombing of Dres-

den. There are rational political, military, legal, and ethical reasons to support the decisions that led to each, but these were identified only after a great deal of research. An individual teaching either ethics or the law of war must have a natural inquisitiveness about history in order to place his topic in perspective.[19]

6. *Recognize the importance of your subject.* The concerns of the American people for morality and legality are regarded by the enemies of the United States as a highly vulnerable center of gravity that must be exploited at every opportunity. Our loss in Vietnam in large measure occurred through the success of North Vietnam repeatedly casting all U.S. operations in terms of their alleged illegality, or the immorality of the war in general. The bombing campaigns over North Vietnam saw the greatest restraint ever offered by a warring nation to minimize collateral civilian casualties. The North Vietnamese responded by alleging massive civilian casualties while using their own civilian population to shield legitimate targets from attack. In the Rolling Thunder campaign, the Johnson administration responded to the North Vietnamese charges by increasing the constraints on U.S. forces or denying authorization to attack legitimate targets in or adjacent to populated areas. The North Vietnamese were able to set the terms of reference for the war, and our national leadership was incapable of responding to or changing those terms of reference.

Today, opponents of U.S. assistance to the democratically elected government in El Salvador and to support for the democratic resistance in Nicaragua couch their opposition in terms of the morality or legality of U.S. efforts. Following the airstrikes in Libya, Libyan officials attempted a similar disinformation effort, asserting massive civilian casualties while denying damage to the terrorist-related targets that were the object of attack. It was disclosed that the alleged death of Muammar Ghadaffi's stepdaughter in the air strike by U.S. Air Force F-111 aircraft on Aziziyah Barracks was a Libyan fabrication. Its purpose was clear: to influence public opinion in the United States and the Western world to forestall further attacks.

Ethics and the law are not always synonymous, but they are compatible in many respects. Not the least of these is their value as a foreign policy tool. Each is extremely important in today's world in assuring the American people of the correctness of a strategic or tactical decision, and leaders at all levels ignore this fact at their peril. We have taken a proactive approach to teaching the law of war by emphasizing this point. The same can be done in teaching other field of ethics.

NOTES

1. The Department of Defense, Joint Chiefs of Staff, Army, and Marine Corps utilize the traditional term "law of war;" the Navy and Air Force prefer the "law of armed conflict." The terms are regarded as synonymous, and are defined as "that part of international law that regulates the conduct of armed hostilities." Joint Chiefs of Staff Publication 1, *Dictionary of Military and Associated Terms* (January 1, 1986). The 1949 treaties are the Geneva Convention for the Amelioration of the Wounded and Sick in Armed Forces in the Field; Geneva Convention for the

Amelioration of the Condition of Wounded, Sick and Ship-wrecked Members of Armed Forces at Sea; Geneva Convention Relative to the Treatment of Prisoners of War; and Geneva Convention Relative to the Protection of Civilian Persons in Time of War.

2. Common article 1 to the four 1949 Geneva Conventions states that "The High Contracting Parties undertake to respect and to ensure respect for the present Convention in all circumstances." At the 1974-1977 Diplomatic Conference that negotiated the two 1977 Protocols Additional to the Geneva Conventions of 1949, the Socialist block adamantly refused to accept any codification of the concept of proportionality. Although a standard was adopted that resembles the concept (without identifying it as such), it is fundamentally flawed and would be constitutionally void for vagueness in its present form. Its negotiation illustrates the difficulty of applying general moral concepts to specific combat situations under all circumstances. Because of this and other substantial military, political, and humanitarian concerns with the highly politicized language of Additional Protocol I, the decision has been taken to forward additional Protocol II only to the United States Senate for its advice and consent to ratification. For discussion of the interrelationship between ethics and the law of war, see Geoffrey Best, *Humanity in Warfare* (1980) and William V. O'Brien, *The Conduct of Just and Limited War* (1981).

3. "Kind-hearted people might, of course, think there was some ingenious way to disarm or defeat an enemy without too much bloodshed and might imagine this is the true goal of the art of war. Pleasant as it sounds, it is a fallacy that must be exposed; war is such a dangerous business that the mistakes which come from kindness are the very worst," Carl von Clausewitz, *On War*, ed. Michael Howard and Peter Paret (Princeton: Princeton University Press, 1976), p. 75.

4. During the 1965-1968 Rolling Thunder air campaign over North Vietnam, Secretary of Defense Robert S. McNamara elected to deny the military the authority to attack other targets only where collateral civilian casualties could be held to an absolute minimum. In some cases he directed attack parameters that placed U.S. aircraft and aircrews at greatest risk in order to hold down collateral civilian casualties. The North Vietnamese re-

sponded by placing all war materials and military units and positions within populated areas and armed the civilian population to create small arms barrages to defeat low-flying U.S. aircraft. Exploitation of the civilian population was so substantial that the ICRC warned the North Vietnamese government that such continued action could subject the entire population of North Vietnam, see the author's "Rolling Thunder and the Law of War," *Air University Review* (January-February 1982), pp. 2-23; and "Linebacker and the Law of War," *Air University Review* (January-February 1983), pp. 2-30.

5. See Guenter Lewy, *America in Vietnam* (New York: Oxford Press, 1978), pp. 366-69; and U.S., Department of the Army, *Report on the Department of the Army Review of the Preliminary Investigations Into the My Lai Incident* (1970). Failure of law of war training was a common factor in most Vietnam-era incidents. See Parks, "Crimes in Hostilities," *Marine Corps Gazette* (August 1976, pp 16-22, and September 1976), pp. 33-39.

6. Department of Defense Directive 5100.7, Subject: DOD Law of War Program. Service directives implementing the DOD directive are Army Regulation 350-216; Air Force Regulation 110-32; Secretary of the Navy Instruction 3300.1A; OPNAVINST 3300.52; and Marine Corps Order 3300.3. In a related program, DOD Instruction 5500.15 requires the review of all new weapons to insure U.S. compliance with its law of war obligations. This directive was the first of its type anywhere in the world.

7. Article 1 of Hague Convention IV of 1907 provides that "The Contracting Parties shall issue instructions to their armed forces which shall be in conformity with the regulations respecting the laws and customs of war on land." The four Geneva Conventions of 1949 each contain a generally common article stating that "The High Contracting Parties undertake, in time of peace as in time of war, to disseminate the text of the present convention[s] as widely as possible in their countries and, in particular, to include the study thereof in their programs of military instruction and, if possible, civil instruction, so that the principles thereof may become known to all their armed forces and to their entire population." While there has been law of war instruction in the United States military for most of this century, no instruction is offered in the civilian sector, although other

nations (such as Australia and Canada) have such programs. The first and only exposure the average citizen has to the law of war is in the military service. Changing views of the relevance of ethics or morality on the battlefield in a brief lecture on the law of war is challenging, at the least; Constitution of the United States, article VI.

8. Lewy, *supra* n. 8, at 367.

9. Others include the principles of war, military doctrine, rules of engagement, commander's instructions, leadership principles, target acquisition methods, communications procedures, and fire support coordination methods. Although this presentation concentrates on the law of war program, military ethics also is discussed in various leadership classes or courses taught within the military.

10. M. MacDougal and F. Feliciano, *Law and Minimum World Public Order* (1961), p. 72; Air Force Manual 1-1, *Functions and Basic Doctrine of the United States Air Force* (1979), p. 5-5, defines economy of force to mean that "no more—or less— effort should be devoted to a task than is necessary to achieve the objective. . . . This phrase implies the correct selection and use of weapon systems, maximum productivity from available flying effort, and careful balance in the allocation of tasks." While this is neither the traditional nor current definition of economy of force, its emphasis on the judicious use of limited assets in the target-rich atmosphere of the modern battlefield shows the consistency with law of war principles urging discrimination in the use of firepower.

11. Headquarters, U.S. Marine Corps, *The U.S. Marine—The Essential Subject* (Marine Corps Order P1550.14D [1983]), p. 1-27. This publication is distributed to every recruit upon entry into the Marine Corps, and is the foundation for his formal education as a Marine.

12. As happened in the brief flurry of shackling and countershackling of Canadian and German prisoners of war following the Dieppe raid. In contrast, German treatment of U.S. and British Commonwealth prisoners of war in World War II, while usually harsh and often brutal, was far better than that of Soviet soldiers for this reason.

13. Nazi abuse made the Soviet population, previously friendly and receptive, hostile. See Alexander Dallin, *German*

Rule in Russia, 1941-1945: A Study of Occupation Politics (1957). Here, however, is where a distinction must be made between a moral democracy and an amoral totalitarian state. While Mao Tse-Tung emphasized the need to respect the civilian population, it was clear that what could not be gained through kindness would be achieved through intimidation. The Viet Cong assassination policy in South Vietnam, Soviet attacks on the civilian population in Afghanistan, the program by the Marxist People's Revolutionary Army factions of the Farabundo Marti National Liberation Front in El Salvador of assassinating democratically elected mayors, and a similar assassination policy by the Maoist Shining Path guerrilla movement in Peru indicate clearly that not all men accept the same moral/legal standards.

14. This effect again is uneven. Despite widespread abuse of the civilian population in Afghanistan by Soviet occupation forces, as reported in the February 1985 report of the United Nations Economic and Social Council, "Report on the Situation of Human Rights in Afghanistan" (E/CN.4/1985/21, February 19, 1985), and two reports by Helsinki Watch (*Tears, Blood and Cries*, December 1984 and *To Die In Afghanistan*, December 1985), the Soviet Union ignored international public opinion and, controlling the flow of information within its own borders, avoided even the most remote possibility of domestic moral anguish. Even within the United States, the standards regarding morality have been applied unevenly. Critics of U.S. support for the democratically elected government of El Salvador have been quick to focus on any shortcoming of that government, actual, alleged, or, in some cases, contrived, but quicker to turn a blind eye to atrocities committed by the rebels, excusing them in the name of "liberation theology." To paraphrase a recent expression, "'liberation theology' is neither."

15. The unit is Headquarters Marine Corps Training Department's Reserve Augmentation Unit (Law of War). After two dozen courses, there is a mathematical probability of 1 in 40 that the commander of a deploying Marine amphibious unit will be a course graduate, 1 in 20 that one of his three element commanders will be a course graduate, better than 1 in 2 that his judge advocate will have attended the course, and a statistical certainty that one of the MAU's 40 officers will have graduated from the course.

As part of the Marine Corps Law of War course, the unit has published a deskbook used in conjunction with course lectures, prepared seminar problems and solutions, and published a comprehensive reference book of sources and materials on the law of war.

Separately, the unit is preparing a correspondence course on the law of war for enlisted Marines and a handbook for commanders similar to the Air Force's excellent AFP 110-34 (25 July 1980). The unit prepared a series of law of war articles that appeared in base newspapers and other Service news sources such as the *Air Force Times*. Unit members are frequent contributors of law of war articles to professional journals such as the *Marine Corps Gazette* and the *Naval Institute Proceedings*. See, for example, Colonel James H. Jeffries III, USMCR, "Marines are Marines are Marines," *Proceedings* 113,1 (January 1987), pp. 117-18.

16. As well as representatives of the Office of the Secretary of Defense, the Joint Chiefs of Staff, service staffs, and the war colleges.

17. MJCS 59-83 (1983), Subject: Implementation of the DOD Law of War Program. A law of war checklist for review of operations plans was prepared by the Marine Corps Reserve law of war unit (fn. 20). The checklist is in use by all major commands and all services.

18. For discussion of the law of war factors considered in the planning and execution of the U.S. mission against Libya, see the author's "Crossing the Line," *Naval Institute Proceedings* 112,11 (November 1986), pp. 40-52.

19. An excellent example of the study of history from the point of view of ethics is Ronald Schaffer's *Wings of Judgment: American Bombing in World War II* (New York: Oxford University Press, 1985).

PART IV

CONTEMPORARY ISSUES IN MILITARY ETHICS

ᡃᡃᠪᠵ᠑ᡁᡳᠪᡝᠨ

THINKING ETHICALLY ABOUT THE STRATEGIC DEFENSE INITIATIVE: SOME PRELIMINARIES

MICHAEL O. WHEELER
Colonel, U.S. Air Force

Colonel Wheeler asks whether moral superiority necessarily attaches to either side in the debate over a defense against ballistic nuclear missiles. To answer the question, he proceeds systematically from an analysis of the ethics of defense in general, to an analysis of defense against nuclear weapons, to an analysis of the ethics of strategic defense against ballistic missiles.

When Harry Truman was president, he displayed a passage from Mark Twain in the Oval Office, "Always do right—this will gratify some and astonish the rest." If Twain's motto were applied new to a strategic defense, there is quite a bit that appears to be clearly and distinctly right. For some, strategic defense offers hope and a way out of the moral anxiety posed by the vision of nuclear deterrence permanently underwritten by the uncertain threat of mutual destruction. For others it offers the prospect of honorably defending against nuclear devastation rather than using weapons of mass destruction. As one finds upon reflection, however, the matter is not that simple. There are strong and compelling arguments on both sides of the debate over the wisdom of the Strategic Defense Initiative (or SDI). Some of those arguments are technical, some are military, some are political, some are legal and even constitutional. And some of the arguments are ethical. This essay will explore preliminaries for thinking ethically about SDI.

To organize the discussion, this examination will proceed through three questions, each of which is slightly narrower than its predecessor. Is there an ethics of defense? Is there an ethics of strategic defense? Is there an ethics of strategic defense against ballistic missiles? As with many ethical matters, understanding the questions may prove as illuminating as attempting the answers.

AN ETHICS OF DEFENSE?

The distinction between offense and defense is as old as war. At tactical, strategic, and grand strategic levels, one can conceptualize what at first appears to be a constructive difference between attacking and defending against attack. Where does that distinction lead?

Consider initially how Kant might treat the matter. Immanuel Kant was one of the first philosophers to attempt to associate the notion of what an act is with the mental state of the actor. His argument as I understand it is that to have moral worth, an act must be done out of respect for that duty which the categorical imperative leads one rationally to choose and do. Hypothetical imperatives are prudential rules. Categorical imperatives are moral rules. Act only according to that maxim by which you can at the same time will that it should become a universal law. Act as though the maxim or your action were by your will to become a universal law of nature. Act so as to treat every rational being as an end in itself and never as a means to an end.

To apply this mode of thought to defense, one must ask whether there is a special, generic act of defending. Kant's insight suggests that an act of defending cannot be understood separate from the mental state of the actor. The following example (reflecting the military folk wisdom that a good defense is a good offense, which Kant would view to be a hypothetical imperative) clarifies this point.

Colonel Joshua Lawrence Chamberlain, a former professor of rhetoric and "natural and revealed religion" at Bowdoin College, orders the weary survivors of the 20th Regiment of Infantry, Maine Volunteers, to fix bayonets and charge down the steep, narrow slopes of the Little Round Top in the midst of a violent battle. The Confederate attack at that tactical point is broken. The Union defensive line holds. In his magnificent recreation of the Gettysburg campaign, Michael Shaara pored through what evidence remains to try to recapture the mental states of the commanders. He describes what he imagines to be Joshua Chamberlain's moment of decision:

> One man said, "Sir, I guess we ought to pull out." Chamberlain said, "Can't do that." Spear: "We won't hold 'em again." Chamberlain: "If we don't hold, they go right on by and over the hill and the whole flank caves in." He looked from face to face. The enormity of it, the weight of the line, was a mass too great to express. But he could see it is as clearly as in a broad wide vision, a Biblical dream: If the line broke here, then the hill was gone, all these boys from Pennsylvania, New York, hit from behind, above. Once the hill went,

the flank of the army went. Good God! He could see troops running: he could see the blue tide, the bloody tide. Kilrain: "Colonel, they're coming." Chamberlain marveled. But we're not so bad ourselves. One recourse. Can't go back. Can't stay where we are. Results: inevitable. The idea formed. "Let's fix bayonets," Chamberlain said.[1]

Joshua Chamberlain ordered an attack. Two hundred men responded. They went on the offensive. But their actions were acts of defense. How does one assess the moral worth of their actions? Rather than work through attempting to apply the categorical imperative, it is helpful for purposes of this essay to broaden the discussion and turn at this point to another perspective: the Just War tradition.

Much of Western thought on the ethics of violence is drawn together in the Just War tradition. Causes, intentions, motivations, circumstances, and consequences are woven into responding to the questions: Is resort to violence justified? What is permitted and what is prohibited once one resorts to violence? *Jus ad bellum* arguments are structured in terms of just cause, proper authority, right intention, proportionality (in an aggregate sense), last resort, and the aim of peace. *Jus in bello* arguments draw upon proportionality (in a more proximate sense) and discrimination (or noncombatant immunity). Both sets of arguments are illuminated by the classic example which Augustine considered to be fundamental: an aggressor in the act of attacking (or about to attack), an innocent victim, and an onlooker. The interplay among these three suggests another perspective on the act of defense.

Return, for a moment, to the events of July 2, 1863, at Gettysburg. It is the second year of a tragic and bloody civil war. Robert E. Lee, one of the most revered military leaders in American history, has assumed command of the Army of Northern Virginia on June 1, 1862, and one year later almost to the day leads seventy thousand men across the Potomac to begin the calculated yet risky invasion of the North. He marches knowing that the Confederacy is prepared to offer Abraham Lincoln peace once Lee destroys the Army of the Potomac. Six months earlier, Lincoln had issued a proclamation declaring that all slaves in areas still in rebellion are "then, henceforward, and forever free." Shaara speculates on Chamberlain's thoughts as the Union and Confederate forces approach one another at Gettysburg.

> Truth is too personal. Don't know if I can express it. He shook his head. I'll wave no more flags for home. No tears for Mother. Nobody ever dies for apple pie. He walked slowly toward the dark grove. He has a complicated brain and there were things going on back there from time to time that he only dimly understood, so he relied on his instincts, but he was learning all the time. The faith itself was simple: he believed in the dignity of man. His ancestors were Huguenots, refugees of a chained and bloody Europe. He has learned their stories in the cradle. He had grown up believing in America and the individual and it was a stronger faith than his faith in God. This was the land where no man had to bow. In this place at last a man could stand up free of the past, free of tradition and blood ties and the curse of royalty and become what he wished to become. . . . The fact of slavery upon this incredibly beautiful new clear earth was appalling.[2]

Chamberlain's decision to attack is set against this background. Hostilities have commenced under proper authority. (Lincoln has called for volunteers on April 12, 1861; Chamberlain has received his commission from the Governor of Maine one year later.) There is ample reason to believe that Chamberlain thought in terms of a demonstrably ethical cause (banning slavery—indeed, Kant's development of the categorical imperative provides one of the most eloquent philosophical frameworks for banning slavery, even so-called freely chosen slavery). The decision to counterattack appears reasonable, given Chamberlain's circumstances, and it was executed in a measured fashion (against armed combatants, with prisoners taken). In short, Chamberlain's act of ordering the bayonet charge has all the marks of an act of defense which has moral worth. But does it serve as ground for generalizing on the ethics of defense?

It already has been suggested that distinguishing between an act of offense and an act of defense is not so simple as may be expected. Even if one attempts to distinguish between an act of *aggression* and an act of *defense* (which appears to be the point of Augustine's example, more fully developed in the brief assessment of Chamberlain's decision), the answer is not so simple. It is not clear, for instance, that Lee's northern campaign was an act of aggression, and that the Confederate attack at Gettysburg thus flowed from either aggressive or less worthy intent than did Chamberlain's actions. The example of Alfred T. Mahan provides perspective in this matter.

Alfred T. Mahan is best known, of course, for his views on naval strategy and geopolitics. Less well known is the fact that late in life, Mahan worked through a number of ethical questions. His father was a West Point professor, well acquainted with the commanders on both sides of the Civil War and especially close to Lee. Professor Mahan and Lee both were Virginians, had served together in the Engineers, had worked to build up West Point. William Puleston describes the anguish that the elder Mahan expressed the day the telegram arrived announcing Lee's decision to resign his commission and join the Confederacy. "He saw Beauregard and others go without comment, but Lee was different. All he could say to his wife was 'Elly—Lee has gone.'"[3]

Alfred T. Mahan (as did his father) stayed with the Union. The younger Mahan in fact began his naval career during the Civil War. He never lost the emotional perspective one gains from knowing, respecting, even longing for those one is fighting. In 1899, Alfred T. Mahan wrote these words:

> One may now see, or think that he sees, as does this writer, with Lincoln, that if slavery is not wrong, nothing is wrong. It is not so clear half a century ago; and while no honor is too great for those early heroes, who for this sublime conviction withstood obloquy and persecution, legal and illegal, it should be never forgotten that the then slave States, in their resolute determination to maintain by arms, if need be, and against superior force, that which they believed to be their constitutional political right, made no small contribution to the record of fidelity to conscience and to duty, which is the highest title of a nation to honor. . . . However the result may afterwards be interpreted as indicated of the justice of a cause—an interpretation always questionable,— a state, when it goes to war, should do so not to test the rightfulness of its claims, but because being convinced in its conscience of that rightfulness, no other means of overcoming evil remains—It is not the accuracy of the decision but the faithfulness to conviction, that constitutes the moral worth of action, national or individual.[4]

One may disagree with Mahan's assessment, but it is difficult to disagree with the proposition that Robert E. Lee was a man of high conscience and conviction, and that both Lee and Chamberlain were convinced of the rightness of their causes, the importance of duty, and the appropriate measure of their means.

Other examples could be chosen; however, I conclude from this discussion that there is no simple distinction between defense and offense, and that defense as we commonly understand it has no prima facie claim to moral superiority over offense. Does shifting the discussion to nuclear weapons modify these conclusions?

AN ETHICS OF STRATEGIC DEFENSE?

Strategic, according to the *Oxford English Dictionary,* is an adjective meaning of or belonging to *strategy,* useful or important in regard to strategy. *Strategy* is derived from the Greek phrase for office or command of a general, or (more broadly) generalship. Since 1945, Western thought (or at least American thought) has gotten away from this military grounding to identify *strategic* not exclusively but certainly closely with questions of grand strategy, and especially with questions of the nuclear balance.

A brief recital of history is appropriate. During World War II the United States developed and used the atomic bomb. Harry Truman became president of the United States on April 12, 1945. Germany surrendered one month later. In July an atomic device that had been under secret development for several years was tested in the New Mexico desert. On 6 and 9 August, in accord with Truman's orders, American air crews dropped the atomic bomb on Hiroshima and Nagasaki, respectively. Truman broadcast a public statement shortly after Nagasaki, threatening Japan with destruction if it did not surrender. Included in that statement was a classic consequentialist defense of the decision to use the bomb: "We have used it in order to shorten the agony of war, in order to save the lives of thousands and thousands of young Americans. We shall continue to use it until we completely destroy Japan's power to make war. Only a Japanese surrender will stop us."[5]

The consequentialist argument (and, more specifically, act utilitarianism) has deep roots in Western thought. The thesis that the rightness or wrongness of an action is determined by the goodness or badness of its consequences is one structure of moral discourse, developed extensively in more recent times by Jeremy Bentham (as hedonistic act utilitarianism) and by John Stuart Mill (whose writings leave unclear whether act or rule utilitarianism best characterizes his thought). What is important, however, is not drawing out the differences among forms of consequentialist argument but considering how consequentialist approaches help in exploring the ethics of strategic defense.

Consider, again, the decision to use the atomic bomb. Was Truman's decision (and the subsequent use) an act of defense or offense? In 1945, Harry Truman ordered the dropping of the atomic bomb. What distinguishes the decisions of Truman in 1945 and of Joshua Chamberlain in 1863?

Both decisions clearly resulted in offensive acts (military attacks), but in neither case is there a clearcut distinction between an offensive and a counteroffensive (nor between offense and defense). Joshua

Chamberlain's decision was narrower (tactical); Truman's, broader (strategic or grand strategic, not in the sense of *strategic* defense but in the more traditional meanings of the term). Truman's decision resulted in action that reasonably could be expected to be less discriminating (employing weapons of mass destruction).

It is not clear that Truman's decision was not an act of defense. He reminded his audience on August 9, 1945, that Pearl Harbor lay behind the chain of events leading to Hiroshima and Nagasaki. One could debate the causal chain; however, it would seem that much the same complex moral analysis that applied to Joshua Chamberlain's bayonet charge would apply to Harry Truman's use of the atomic bomb, as applied to questions of offense and defense. Or to put it another way, it is not evident that a decision involving nuclear weapons fundamentally alters the thesis advanced in the preceding section that defense does not have a prima facie, superior claim to moral worth. What, however, of a defense *against* the use of nuclear weapons? Does that shift the argument? Is there a prima facie case for the moral worth of strategic defense against nuclear attack?

Had the Japanese Air Force not been devastated by August 1945, it could (at least in theory) have intercepted the B-29s carrying atomic weapons to attack Japan and destroyed the bombers before they reached their targets. Success in mounting such a defense is highly conjectural. The size of the nuclear stockpiles (then very small), the extent and promptness of Japanese intelligence (identifying which bombers to target), the skill of Japanese air crews, and blind chance (in such things as weather) would enter into the picture, as would the most elementary consideration—surprise (Japan appears not to have known that America had an atomic bomb). The point is that one can conceive of circumstances in 1945 in which Japan could have attempted to defend against atomic attack. Would such strategic defenses have a prima facie claim to moral worth, superior to the claims that led to use of the atomic bomb? It is hard to envision what would constitute such a prima facie claim.

As a more practical matter, what made arguments of strategic defense as problematic then as now is the recognition that even a single weapon could effect mass destruction. There was no way then, and may never be a way, to guarantee that a single nuclear weapon (or a few nuclear weapons) cannot penetrate strategic defenses. A surprise or stealthy nuclear attack, a massed nuclear attack, a precursor attack against defenses—these and other possibilities will continue to influence military assessment of the subject of the strategic nuclear offense-defense relationship. Those considerations were present at the start of the nuclear age. It is out of such a calculus that the doctrine of strategic deterrence was born. One need not revisit the detailed evolution of East-West relations after 1945, nor the increasing sophistication of atomic weapons and their delivery systems, nor the growth of strategic stockpiles, nor the proliferation of nuclear weapons to other nations to appreciate why strategic defense, although never rejected totally, failed to dominate American defense policy. The question was one of success— and how to measure it. As Father John Courtney

Murray reminds us, "Policy is the meeting-place of the world of power and the world of morality, in which there takes place the concrete reconciliation of the duty of success that rests upon the statesman and the duty of justice that rests upon the civilized nation that he serves."[6] Harry Truman and his successors grappled with how one reconciles preventing nuclear attack with the possession of nuclear weapons (or, as the alliance structures evolved after 1945, with preventing nonnuclear war on the scale of the World Wars).

Strategic deterrence is based upon the threat certain to be made to an adversary that if he initiates aggression, he cannot pursue it and prevail (by nuclear means or by conventional means escalating to a deliberately vague threshold) by any reasonable standards. What ultimately underwrites that threat is nuclear weapons.

If one accepts the soundness of the arguments that strategic deterrence based upon the credible threat to use nuclear weapons prevents nuclear aggression and contributes to prevention of large-scale nonnuclear aggression, then one would appear to reject the claim that strategic defenses have either a prima facie moral worth or a morally superior position to a strategic offense. Here, however, the argument becomes quite complex. Can nuclear weapons ever be used in a just cause or in a proportionate way? Would their very use render invalid the grounds for advancing the justice of one's claims? These are fundamental questions.

THINKING ETHICALLY ABOUT THE SDI

AN ETHICS OF STRATEGIC DEFENSE
AGAINST BALLISTIC MISSILES?

Although chemically powered missiles are centuries old, German efforts at Peenemunde in World War II to rush into service the A-4 rocket (more commonly known as the V-2) resulted in a dramatic new military threat, the modern ballistic missile. The Germans commenced their V-2 campaign against England shortly after 6:00 p.m. on September 8, 1944, with an attack on Chiswick, a suburb of London. This V-2 (and nine others that landed in England over the next six days) were launched from the continent, some 190 miles distant. Their flight times were less than five minutes. The first week's casualties from V-2 attacks numbered 187—22 killed, 68 seriously injured, and 97 slightly injured. By the end of the war, more than 25,000 V-weapons (the V-2 and the V-1, a forerunner of the modern cruise missile) hit targets in England and on the European continent. In England alone, V-weapons caused over 30,000 casualties.[7]

By modern standards, the V-2 was a primitive system. At distances of 190 to 220 miles, accuracy was low; V-2 range errors averaged 14 miles and line errors 7.5 miles. The energy packed into 1,600 pounds of conventional high explosive delivered by a V-2 dug craters 34.5 feet in diameter and 9.5 feet deep. The V-2 campaign sparked intensive study by the British Anti-Aircraft Command of possible means of defending against rocket attack. One plan explored the feasibility of massing artillery fire at or near the end of the V-2 flight corridor. The plan was rejected as infeasible—it required firing 320,000 28-

lb antiaircraft shells to destroy a single V-2. Another report recommended that "all other possible countermeasures should be explored, particularly the use of guided counter-missiles."[8]

Almost forty years span the time from when the British military staff at Glenthorn in Stanmore began debating how to defend against V-2 attack and when President Reagan announced from the Oval Office that his administration would seek to develop a defense against ballistic missiles through the Strategic Defense Initiative. In the 1970s the United States briefly deployed an operational ballistic missile defense in the northeast corner of North Dakota, on the edges of the ballistic missile field at Grand Forks. This SAFEGUARD system employing older technologies could not effectively defend against ballistic missile attack and was largely dismantled. The issue posed by President Reagan on March 23, 1983, briefly touched on the issue of the feasibility of applying new technologies to ballistic missile defense. As he presented his central themes, however, the president shifted to a more fundamentally moral note:

> Over the course of these discussions [with my advisors], I've become more and more deeply convinced that the human spirit must be capable of rising above dealing with other nations and human beings by threatening their existence. . . . Tonight, consistent with our obligations of the ABM Treaty and recognizing the need for closer consultation with our allies, I'm taking an important first step. I am directing a comprehensive and intensive effort to define a long-term research and development program to begin to achieve our ultimate goal of eliminating the threat posed by strategic nuclear missiles. . . . My fellow Americans, tonight we're launching an effort which holds the promise of changing the course of human history.[9]

It has been argued that defense as we commonly understand it has no prima facie claim to moral superiority over offense and that even placing the argument in the context of nuclear weapons does not alter this proposition. But what of defense against nuclear weapons delivered by ballistic missiles? Does this alter the argument?

What is unique about ballistic missile attack is not the certainty with which a weapon can be delivered nor the short time of flight, nor the yield or accuracy, nor the lack of a defense. One can envision circumstances in which other delivery systems can give high assurance of delivering a weapon on target. Supersonic (and perhaps hypersonic) delivery vehicles other than ballistic missiles are technically feasible; other weapons are equally accurate and have at least as much yield, and SDI holds out high promise of identifying feasible defenses against ballistic missiles for the future. The uniqueness of the ballistic missile inventories at this point in time is they offer a *practical* means of maintaining a high-confidence posture responsive to national command and capable of assuring a weapon could be delivered and destroy a target within a matter of minutes. It is from this fact that one can argue that there is indeed inherent in these circumstances an issue of human spirit. War is a political act subject to political decision. The threat of ballistic missile attack reduces the time for decision to a matter of minutes and perhaps even seconds. That renders the chances of an informed, rational decision highly problematic. Whether one takes a Kantian or Consequentialist point of view, the answer seems equally clear. Moral decisionmaking under such conditions is reduced more to instinct than reason, which calls into question whether conditions for reaching a morally sound decision would in fact exist.

The dramatic compression of the time for deciding whether to respond to an attack by ballistic missiles armed with nuclear weapons is deeply disturbing. However, even here, the weight of evidence to establish a clear, prima facie argument in favor of defense is missing. As before, questions of intent and consequences, or just cause and proper authority, or proportionality, and of last resort are brought to bear.

One can conceive of other moral decision frameworks (including many in warfare) where time for decision is measured in minutes or seconds. But we do not conclude in those instances that there is a prima facie case for a particular decision. Rather, we subject a decision to ethics criteria. I conclude that the same complex moral process that allows a rational person to work through the rightness or wrongness of other human actions applies to discussing the ethical implications of warfare, of nuclear weapons, and of defense against ballistic missiles. This is a modest but not a trivial conclusion. There is enough popular exposition surrounding SDI to remind ourselves of the value of careful, deliberate reasoning, and especially of the timeless advice of John Locke that "it is ambition enough to be employed as an under-laborer in clearing the ground a little."[10] To clear the ground a little, we must deal with some of the preliminaries that precede a more thorough assessment of the ethical implications of SDI.

NOTES

1. Michael Shaara, *The Killer Angels* (New York: Ballantine Books, 1974), p. 230.

2. Ibid., p. 27.

3. Captain W. D. Puleston, USN, *Mahan: The Life and Work of Captain Alfred Thayer Mahan* (New Haven: Yale University Press, 1939), p. 30.

4. Alfred T. Mahan, "The Moral Aspect of War, "*The North American Review* (October 1899), reprinted in Mahan, *Some Neglected Aspects of War* (Boston: Little, Brown, and Company, 1970). The cited passage is at pages 29-30.

5. Truman's radio statement of 9 August 1945 is reprinted as Appendix 3 in the Department of State publication *International Control of Atomic Energy: Growth of a Policy* (Washington, D.C.: U.S. Government Printing Office, 1947). The cited passage is at page 107.

6. John Courtney Murray, S.J., "Morality and Modern War," reprinted in *The Moral Dilemma of Nuclear Weapons: Essays from Worldview* (New York: The Council on Religion and International Affairs, 1961). The cited passage is at page 15.

7. The information on the V-2 program and campaign is taken from Frederick I. Ordway, III, and Mitchell R. Sharpe, *The Rocket Team* (Cambridge, Mass: The MIT Press, 1979), pp 223-39.

8. Ibid., p. 231.

9. President Reagan's 23 March 1983 Speech on Defense Spending and Defensive Technology can be found in *Weekly Compilation of Presidential Documents*, vol. 19, no. 12 (Monday, March 28, 1983), pp. 423-66.

10. John Locke, *An Essay Concerning Human Understanding*, vol. 1, compiled and annotated by Alexander Campbell Fraser (New York: Dover Publications, Inc., 1959), p. 14.

SMALL WARS AND MORALLY SOUND STRATEGY

H.F. KUENNING
Major, U.S. Army

Major Kuenning explains why our adversaries in small wars have often succeeded in portraying themselves as occupying the moral high ground. With patience and thoughtfulness, he shows that the American tendency to think of our wars as holy crusades has inhibited our willingness to commit forces to small wars, and has led us to fight those wars with the kinds of massively destructive weapons that make our adversaries seem small and virtuous by comparison.

Soldiers face the continuing prospect of fighting limited conflicts around the world in the name of U.S. interests. In these conflicts, one of the most important but often over-looked keys to successful outcomes is the morality of the strategic and operational conduct of the war. Perceptions of the morality of U.S. operations will affect whether, how, and for how long we are allowed to fight. The perceptions that count are those of the American public, our soldiers, and to a lesser degree, the rest of the free world. Criticism of the Vietnam war was couched in distinctly moral terms. And criticism came from a broad spectrum of American institutions and citizens, not just an irresponsible minority.

H.F. KUENNING

THE AMERICAN JUST WAR TRADITION
AND SMALL WARS

The relation of moral values to military strategy and operations may not seem critical to military officers conditioned to leave political and social considerations to civilian leaders, but that perception is both irresponsible and dangerous. Some argue that war is inherently immoral (or amoral), that "clean fighting" is a contradiction in terms, or that unacceptable noncombatant targeting, death, and destruction are inevitable elements of modern warfare. Americans who take these positions ignore the importance of moral values in our culture and national policies. They also give up an American strategic strength, the moral "high ground."

Key questions for future wars are (1) Can the United States win? (2) Can we win and act morally? and (3) Must we act morally in order to win? Some answers are at hand. If U.S. forces cannot fight with substantially Western moral values and maintain in the U.S. public a prevailing opinion that they are doing so, then we likely will lose the next war. Unfortunately, military tradition, doctrine, and force structure present the strong possibility we will fight an immoral and ineffective war. We ignore the strategic value of morality to our peril.

To come to an understanding of the moral problems U.S. forces face in fighting small, limited wars, we must first comprehend the Western Just War tradition, which represents two thousand years of religious, secular, and military thought about the justice of war. The justice *of* war, or deciding whether waging war is morally acceptable, is termed *jus ad bellum*. Justice *in* war, or fighting cleanly, is termed *jus in bello*. Both can be codified in general terms: for *jus ad bellum*, use diplomacy as much as possible to avoid war, fight only at the direction of a legitimate authority, and fight only for very important reasons. For *jus in bello*, fight with efficiency to do what must be done but minimize destruction and suffering.

The Just War principles are generally, if unconsciously, accepted as practical moral principles by Americans, and they represent Western values with respect to international relations, sovereignty of states, human rights, and the value of human life and property. In any conflict, prudent U.S. policy makers evaluate *jus ad bellum* standards of the justice of intervention, the relative value of the geopolitical goals for which we fight, the danger of escalation to unacceptably violent warfare, and the legitimacy of the enemy's political authority. *Jus in bello* standards, however, involve discrimination (engaging only appropriate military targets) and proportion (using only the minimum force necessary to achieve legitimate military goals). In a critical corollary to proportion, some collateral damage or unintended noncombatant death, injury, and destruction is expected in war, but it obviously must be minimized.

Both *jus ad bellum* and *jus in bello* standards are deeply ingrained in traditional American values, but both are in trouble. As war has changed, the tradition has evolved. In the twentieth century, the shifts in warfare have been traumatic, causing a dramatic heightening of *jus ad bellum* standards, which today "outlaw" war. This shift ironically has acted to lower *jus in bello* standards. Thus, failed attempts by Western societies, particularly the United States, to eliminate war have acted to make war more destructive and brutal.

The heightening of *jus ad bellum* standards is an attack on traditional use of war as an international political instrument, as a *legitimate* instrument, at least. This heightening is a response to the continuing development of modern total war, begun with the mobilization of an entire state under the French Revolution, furthered by the bloodbath of World War I, and brought to a culmination in the worldwide holocaust of World War II. Modern wars have demonstrated a growing tendency of societies to take the war to an entire enemy population. Technology has overcome pre-industrial economic and environmental restraints on war, and the advent of nuclear weapons presents the genuine possibility of rapid, worldwide destruction of entire societies. These prospects of worldwide suffering and potential for mass destruction are understandably incompatible with Western values. Thus, *any* justification for *any* war, however small, is seen by world and U.S. policies as movement along a continuum towards a holocaust. Therefore, any war may be immoral since it contains the seeds of the use of nuclear weapons or waging of global war. All warfare since 1945, including that in which the nuclear powers have participated energetically, has been non-nuclear, limited, and conventional, but alarmists are not comforted. The fear of escalation is a moral "trump card" that tends to frustrate any attempts to justify any war.

A second source of heightened *jus ad bellum* standards is the domination of the Western Just War tradition by humanitarian and apolitical ideals proposing a natural state of peace among men, based on relationships above the dirty and amoral realm of governments and politics. Historical American geographic security and two hundred years of liberal democracy, stressing the value and rights of the individual, have bred a dominant American antiwar idealism. Coupled with another American tradition, distrust of government and the military, these ideals have produced perennial political and public confusion over the necessity of using U.S. armed forces in foreign relations. Antiwar sentiment is not a post-Vietnam phenomenon but dates to the eighteenth century. Contemporary American *jus ad bellum* standards (shared in part now by many societies influenced by American liberal democracy) represent a predictable response to a strong peacetime military and superpower confrontation.

These impractical and ideal Just War standards paradoxically undermine *jus in bello*. Idealists who could not justify a war for amoral, political reasons justified war for ultimate moral principles in the past. Thus, the traditional American pacifist quickly can become belligerent crusader. To justify politically necessary or advisable armed force, American political leaders must use idealistic, crusading rhetoric, leading to a "decoupling" of public policy and strategy from the realities of the politics and social systems in the conflict. In a major war, crusading rhetoric may have some use, since the United States may be fighting for ultimate stakes, but in a small war it is a different matter. The slogans reveal the impractical, decoupling nature of American Just War standards: "Make the world safe for democracy," "The War to end all wars," "End the Red menace," "Win the hearts and minds," and even in tiny Grenada, "Protect the vital national security of the United States."

This drive for extreme justification of American intervention endangers *jus in bello* standards of discrimination and proportion, since crusaders are noble warriors facing an evil enemy. Americans tend to view as legitimate a war with a quick decisive, punitive victory. Once American forces are comitted, concern for preserving *American* lives, impatience for a quick resolution, hatred for the evil enemy, and ignorance of the true political and military nature of the conflict combine to hinder a practical, long term, restrained U.S. participation in a small war. Americans, therefore, as humanitarian as their impulses are, often will sanction extreme measures on the part of their armed forces. The results include indiscriminate tactical and strategic bombing, massive use of artillery to preserve American lives, and an attitude that there can be no logical restraints on combat operations. As the war inevitably enters a protracted phase, these practices may backfire, providing evidence of the immorality of American intervention, as crusading ideals give way to the political reality they cover.

It is appalling that American armed forces should operate in highly political limited wars without regard for the impact of their operations on the societies for which the contest is being waged. Yet that pattern is evident in World War II, Korea, and Vietnam. American ideals are not going to change; American presidents will continue to use crusading rhetoric to justify war to the American Congress and public. The American public will continue to justify military force only for idealistic priorities. The key in this problem is the link between *jus ad bellum* and *jus in bello*. As military leaders, thinkers, strategists, or force structure experts, we can have little impact on *jus ad bellum* arguments. When, where, and why U.S. forces are committed is the province of politicians. However, *how* forces fight is almost solely our responsibility. It should be evident that high standards of *jus ad bellum* will not prevent war; a "natural" peace lies only in a mythical future. Military leaders, then, must ensure that *jus in bello*, the morality of our strategy and tactics, is preserved, so that U.S. forces fight more effectively for low-key sustainability and resolution and so that moral criticism of American intervention has less justification.

THE MORAL CLIMATE OF SMALL WARS

The term *small wars* avoids the semantic difficulties of *low-intensity*, since such conflict has been "intense," even on theater-wide levels in Vietnam and Korea. The nature of small wars and the unique relation of U.S. superpower status to that nature raises the potential for special moral problems. Whether U.S. forces are actively involved in combat operations to support a Third World ally, unilaterally employed, or involved in noncombat operations, some of the moral problems will be present.

The first significant source of our moral problems resides in the domination of all other belligerents by U.S. military power, although political goals may not be coherent with those of even U.S. allies. The other belligerent may be fighting for local concerns and the United States for regional or global reasons. The war from a U.S. perspective will be "limited" but "total" to some or all of the local belligerents. The implications for a resulting mismatch of political and military commitment, resolve, or will are obvious. North and South Vietnam waged a total war; we lacked the will to alter decisively the result. Yet U.S. military power set the style and intensity of the war.

Involvement by the United States guarantees that U.S. geopolitical rhetoric will permeate policy and strategy. Designed to justify U.S. intervention (both to domestic and international audiences), the "language" of the war may ignore the true concerns of the local belligerent. With U.S. rhetoric unhinged from the realities of the war, our strategy may follow. Thus, for example, Vietnam in part became a U.S. war fought for U.S. concerns, rather than a Vietnamese war fought with U.S. assistance for South Vietnamese goals.

Another source of small war moral problems is that local antagonisms, despite U.S. rhetoric and ignorance, define the true *causes belli*. In the Third World, fervent religious, ethnic, racial, tribal or political factions probably underlie the modern labels of "ally," neutral, "democracy," "Marxist-Leninist," and so on. These factors exist in all wars, but in a small war they cannot be ignored as easily as when great powers clash. Since local antagonisms may have ancient roots, small wars are unlikely to be brief. Long-term involvement by U.S. forces will result.

Thus, the nature of a small war calls into question the conventional U.S. military approach to a conflict. The local political and social fine points that

U.S. strategists ignored in large wars loom large in a small war for two reasons: first, belligerent success or failure will be determined by how those fine points fall out, and second, the American people's involvement in a small war is based on different concerns, thus raising to public attention and strategic importance issues submerged in large wars. The most important of these moral concerns are the protection of international boundaries, the loss of American lives, the proper use of U.S. budget funds, and, most important in the long run, the heightened importance of protecting noncombatants. Collateral damage, refugees, hunger, human rights, even ecological concerns, become *strategically* important, often overshadowing geopolitical issues. The "enemy" may be a partial combatant, a paramilitary without traditional skills, training, or values who is operating secretly in a "sea" of noncombatants. "Battlefields" may be ill-defined, as a weak enemy avoids confrontation with powerful allied units. Conventional operations to "find, fix, and destroy" the enemy may produce unwanted escalation in nonmilitary arenas: political, congressional, economic, propagandistic, and certainly moral ones.

In such a scenario, as was made evident in Vietnam, poorly defined political/military goals leave conventional military forces in the frustrating and dangerous dilemma of wielding overwhelming force without clear objectives.

In these confusing wars, the importance of developing morally sound strategy stems in great part from the guerrilla's natural moral advantage. The small-war enemy partially offsets his military weakness by appearing to fight a more just war. The moral onus in a small war is on the United States; the moral "advantage" is almost wholly the guerilla's.

In *jus ad bellum* terms, all three requirements for a Just War lean to the position of the guerrilla: fighting as a last resort, acting from legitimate authority, and having a morally justified cause. The weakness of the revolutionary works to his advantage, as he acts the David to the U.S. Goliath. His obvious lack of economic or political alternatives contrasts with vast U.S. economic and political resources. Western restraints on using force only as a last resort present an almost insurmountable barrier for U.S. policy-makers. The guerrilla's legitimacy often stems from his idealistic ideology, particularly Marxist-Leninism. Although lacking political legitimacy or military strength the guerrilla in the twentieth century can draw on powerful Western intellectual sentiment for "liberation movements." The United States is a *status quo* power, often supporting regimes with ties to colonial structures or policies, which often lack the democratic ideals and practices Americans will support. The result may be a *de facto* distrust of U.S. intentions and acceptance of enemy propaganda, giving the guerrilla legitimacy and moral justification. Even when the United States is supporting a guerrilla group seeking to overthrow a demonstratively oppressive regime, as with the Contras in Nicaragua, the U.S. position may be mistrusted and the moral rectitude assigned to the enemy.

In *jus in bello* terms, the appearance of both discrimination and proportionality are difficult for U.S. forces to maintain, but easy for the guerrilla. Some insurgents, particularly the Marxist-Leninists, are skilled at merging political and military goals and controlling the public image of the war. They skillfully use limited military means to serve specific political ends, while the United States tends to divorce military strategy from political issues. Public scrutiny of U.S. operations via media reporting contrasts strongly with the secrecy of enemy organization, planning, and operations. The horror of war, broadcast and critiqued daily, tends to be blamed on the stronger, more visible, forces. Combined with skillful media manipulation by a centrally controlled enemy propaganda machine, this visibility-secrecy contrast becomes a powerful advantage for the guerrilla. In Vietnam, allegations of U.S. war crimes became a virtual "industry" of deceit and staging for an American audience predisposed to distrust its government and abhor the suffering of war. That U.S. atrocities were few, unsystematic, and often officially punished was almost irrelevant to this issue. In the information war, the guerrilla easily presented himself as weak and desperate, fighting for his people's rights.

Ironically, moral analysts side with conventional strategists, tending to blame the guerrilla for the excessive collateral damage and atrocities of small wars.[1] It is the guerrilla who chooses to hide among the population, thus making them targets; conventional units are forced to engage the enlarged "target" to be effective at all. Obviously when discriminating between innocent and enemy becomes more difficult, in a small war, proportionality must be weighted more heavily. Restraint of force must be the rule. Conventional units do not do this well, tending to apply more force in frustration, increasing noncombatant death and injury. Nonmilitary means become more important as employment of military units becomes strategically risky. Only by using effective political and economic tools can U.S. forces overcome the moral advantage of the guerrilla.

MORAL LOGIC IN SMALL WARS

Understanding the moral logic used to condemn or justify military strategies and different forms of fighting "clean" or "dirty" can be difficult because these ethical argument are not often explicit. Rapidly shifting international tensions often create crises between peoples of different cultures and moral value systems. How do morally responsible Americans react when faced with different moral value systems? Can American forces develop and execute morally sound strategy alongside allies of varying cultures, races, and moral values? How do American values apply in different types of war?

The first problem in moral logic may be termed "moral relativism," implying here that immoral enemy or allied behavior calls for American forces to respond immorally in retaliation or reprisal. Sometimes expressed as the argument that no rules exist in war, this common position seems to assume two concepts. Since others' values are different, ours must be invalid, and it is strategically wise or necessary to fight dirty. The alternative, maintaining traditional Western Just War standards in the face of an immoral enemy, is argued to impose unfair restrictions on U.S. forces, to tie their hands.

Yet, facing an enemy who disregards the international law of war and uses noncombatants, mass reprisals, and execution and torture of prisoners need not compel a like response. Indeed, American values and media scrutiny virtually guarantee that even sporadic or accidental immoral military action by U.S. forces may be strategically disastrous. American citizens, especially over a sustained period, will become outraged and soldiers may be morally repulsed causing degradation of morale and discipline. The law of war does authorize reprisals but not in kind; it is illegal for American forces to summarily execute or torture helpless people under any circumstances. It is difficult, moreover, to find any arguments for the strategic wisdom of fighting "dirty"; rather, the opposite would seem to hold true in a small war. Thus, a moral "disjunction" may exist in a small war, but our moral values may be treated as absolutes without loss of strategic leverage or logic.

A second moral logic common to all military forces, but particularly damaging for U.S. forces in small wars, is parochialism. American fighting men tend to treat foreign people in war, friend and foe, with distrust and contempt. This tendency damages cooperation with allies, but more important, it exacerbates American tendencies to fight punitively rather than pragmatically. Our belief in the ultimate value of human life should result in morally sensitive strategies. In small wars, where restraint is also strategically wise, we logically should minimize collateral damage, but the opposite occurs. The lives that our strategies seek to protect are usually American lives. We employ massive, high-tech firepower to obliterate enemy resistance from a distance. But Korea and

Vietnam clearly symbolize this tendency, especially in Korea where civilian casualties nearly equalled military. In a small war, Americans at home and in the service cannot reconcile the loss of American lives with obscure and limited gains in a long, political war.

The final moral logic that operates to the detriment of U.S. forces is the "sliding scale" of moral judgment—actions that go unnoticed in a large war elicit moral outrage in a small war without logical reference to the law of war or moral context of the actions. Wars seen as justified in *jus ad bellum* terms, such as World War II and Korea, tend to be evaluated more leniently in *jus in bello* terms. Wars questionable in *jus ad bellum* terms are strictly evaluated in *jus in bello* terms. In World War II, incendiary bombing of entire cities and use of napalm and flame-throwers were largely uncondemned. Carefully controlled strategic bombing in Vietnam produced few civilian casualties in comparison to the destructive potential: 1,400 in the 1972 B-52 Christmas bombing of Hanoi. Violent public outrage resulted. Napalm, a legal weapon, became a virtual symbol of American atrocity in Vietnam, and was condemned improperly as responsible for thousands of civilian casualties it did not produce.

In a small war, perceptions of U.S. and allied *jus ad bellum* and *jus in bello* violations will tend to feed on each other, as critics search for evidence to bolster arguments for American withdrawal. The unfortunate result may be unfounded but widely believed allegations of American atrocities, criticism of military actions without regard for the realities of war, political and public turmoil, and alienation of the military from public and informed debate. The services thus may be cut off from critical civilian and political sources of moral judgment and support they need to conduct a restrained and practical war.

All of these problems in moral logic underlie American problems with small wars—*jus ad bellum* standards adversely affecting *jus in bello*, the distracting influence of American public opinion, and tradition-bound amoral military approaches to war.[2] These undesirable consequences may be minimized only through farsighted and sound military training designed to maintain discipline and restraint in ambiguous situations, when units must operate under complex, frustrating, and inconsistent political control.

The moral problems of small wars should be examined in the context of genuine U.S. attempts to fight with moral awareness and restraint, for both morally and strategically practical reasons. Although Vietnam elicited tremendous moral outrage in domestic and international politics, it can be argued that the U.S. military attempted to impose unprecedented moral restraints on its units. The planned atrocities of other armies in the twentieth century provide a measure of perspective on how strong is the tendency of Americans to fight justly. Numerous acts of war contrast starkly with the American approach to small wars: the Nazi war crimes; Japanese mistreatment of American POWs; multiple examples of deliberate and systematic atrocities in numerous small wars by the French in Algeria, Idi Amin in Uganda, and the Viet Cong in Vietnam; routine communist torture and manipulation of POWs and apparent Soviet reprisals and atrocities in Afghanistan.

In Vietnam, constant presidential attempts to negotiate an end of the war, frequent publishing of rules engagement and the laws of land warfare, command warnings to avoid noncombatant casualties and respect the Vietnamese civilian population, and trials and convictions of U.S. servicemen for offenses that were, in essence, war crimes, are testimony to typical American attempts at restraint. That some of the reasons for this restraint were pragmatic and strategic, rather than purely moral, only argues that point more forcefully; moral concerns must be considered in developing sound strategy.[3]

Yet American forces are not organized, equipped, or trained to fight with moral sensibility or restraint; a simple desire to fight cleanly cannot overcome the inertia of the "American way of war." Military necessity has canceled moral arguments in all U.S. wars. Humanitarian concerns coupled with American warfighting techniques prevent only wanton cruelty and destruction.[4] In politically and socially sensitive wars, that exclusion is not enough.

THE U.S. MILITARY AND SMALL WARS: INSTITUTIONAL PROBLEMS

Despite a two-hundred year history rich in fighting unconventional limited wars, the U.S. Army, our primary small war service, today reflects that tradition in virtually no organizations, traditions, or doctrines. The great-power status of the United States, her major warfare experience from the Civil War onward, and forty years of confrontation with the USSR have created a military institution (including all four services) unsuited for the special moral problems of small wars. The U.S. military has little basis in professional tradition, organization, equipment, or training to allow us to understand the moral problems of such wars, much less avoid their dangerous strategic and public relations consequences.

The central professional tradition of the U.S. officer corps is the "warrior ethic." The officer corps is not politically oriented citizen soldiers; the officer corps strives to be a politically honorable instruments of the executive (civilian) arm of government, responsible for national security, dedicated to lives of service. The ethic differs from dominant American intellectual liberal traditions. In becoming consciously apolitical and withdrawing from "civilian" ways of thinking, the "warriors" view their proper role as purely military affairs. "Combat," with "victory" the goal is the medium through which the warrior" fulfills his profession's *raison d'etre*, the preservation of the nation. They leave official determination of why and when to fight to civilian leaders responsible for (and capable of) working through the ambiguous "politics" of the situation. They view the "military solution," when implemented, as a relative, definite answer to a politico-military problem.[5] The U.S. officer, then, tends to be unaware of the importance of local politics, economics, and social systems in small wars and also is insensitive to the implications of the deep, nonmilitary impact that military actions (or even the presence) of our units may have on the tactical and strategic outcome of a small war.

A second problem of the "warrior" in small wars is the nature of the enemy. Warriors are trained to engage other warriors in combat, who will organize, equip, and operate in ways the U.S. officer corps understands. The small war enemy may be unprofessional, uninformed, and operate outside the effective comprehension of conventional doctrine and tactics. More significant, the small war enemy may (and likely will) integrate messy social values (religious, ethnic, political) into his operational art, to the dismay of the apolitical U.S. professional.

Useful moral strengths of the code of the U.S. officer include integrity, honor, and service, which do help to develop a relatively restrained approach to war, one responsive to civilian political direction. However, "managerial" techniques and the insidious characteristics of the military bureaucracy further hinder a moral approach to small wars. The need to maintain a large standing force within fluctuating fiscal bounds has produced a search for sound management in the military. American business methods continue to persist in the peacetime military, often diverting all levels of command from the essentials of leadership, future strategy, ethics, and doctrine development. Battalion commanders struggle with a "budget" for their operations, training, and maintenance. Some division commanders oversee daily the minutiae of training ammunition accounts or vehicle "down" time. A commander's success is often viewed in terms of quantifiable indicators, such as UCMJ actions, spare parts on hand, AWOLs, awards, and so forth. Routinely exhausting, overlong duty days and short-term crisis management become the norm for junior and senior officers and noncommissioned officers, who have little time or incentive to pay more than lip service to the invisible, nonquantifiable, deep qualities of a unit's doctrinal, ethical, or professional health.

The "management" of the Vietnam war represented the immoral consequences of using business practices to achieve "victory" in a dirty, politically and socially complex small war. Numbers measured success and progress, as in bombs dropped, sorties flown, villages pacified, weapons captured, and most notoriously, bodies counted. A commander's performance often was tied to such numbers, driving some to inflate reports and certainly inciting greater disregard for discriminate and proportional use of firepower. Management by such internal "bean counting" failed to evaluate properly the impact of military action on the noncombatants.[6]

We have learned some of these lessons and greater emphasis on leadership, professional development of subordinates and moral values is evident throughout the services, but the reorientation is not deep enough. The moral problems of the next small war will be solved or ignored by the young leaders we are developing today. They will be the *de facto* front-line political agents of the United States. Their awareness of the sensitivity of that role will come only from specific, early, and continued education, yet they still are taught by their daily duties that there is no time to reflect, read professionally, or discuss the social, political, and ethical issues of war. What counts is getting that vehicle "up," the report sent, the mess hall cleaned, *today!*

These orientation problems are exacerbated by bureaucratic tendencies found in all large, complex organizations: avoidance of responsibility, use of rules to protect "turf," conformity, careerism, dogmatic adherence to "right thinking," and reliance on a no-risk "safe style." Particularly deadening to the moral sensitivity of combat forces in a small, dirty war, bureaucratic impulses cause us to look *inward* to the needs and norms of our institutions, rather than *outward* to the requirements of the conflict. Small wars require flexibility and the willingness to take risks with new doctrine and strategies.

Conventional force structure and training add to the problem. The great preponderance of the U.S. force structure is designed and trained to fight the USSR in a major conventional war for ultimate stakes. We therefore emphasize traditional "annihilation" or "attrition" strategies relying on massive firepower. Even non-NATO "light" forces, such as the Army's light infantry division, are designed for rapid deployability rather than true low-intensity effectiveness; all have major conventional contingency missions, and so-called "low-intensity doctrine" has been slow to build on painful lessons of the past.[7] All U.S. combat units still are trained to "find, fix, and destroy" enemy units to achieve victory.

Any attempt to use the massive might of a NATO-oriented force in a small war would tend to reproduce the Vietnam experience, wherein the enemy chose consistently the time and place of battle and, thus, the casualty rate he could bear, nullifying our attrition strategy. Even if the enemy had large conventional forces, as in Vietnam, a generally conventional strategy has social, political, and moral effects beyond our current ability to control them or assess them correctly.[8]

There are specific sources of moral problems in the conventional orientation of our forces. One source is the U.S. reliance on high-tech weapons, stemming naturally from the United States' scientific and industrial strengths. American commanders are trained to use sophisticated weapons not only to maximize firepower ("more bang for the buck"), but also to preserve American lives ("trading firepower for bayonets"). Yet such weapons, best exemplified by U.S. air forces (but seen in almost all U.S. combat units), present a troubling image of "technological over-kill." The outrage resulting from tactical and strategic bombing in Vietnam was in part caused by a perception that high-technology weapons are automatically "disproportionate" and often indiscriminate. Using fighter-bombers, rocket-firing attack helicopters, and B-52s against a poorly armed peasant enemy, however carefully controlled, presents a poor public image of U.S. "limited" combat. Combat may need to be intense, but U.S. forces often were not controlled well. Our doctrine relies heavily on combining air power with land power. Long-running arguments by air strategists for the decisiveness of strategic bombing make it unlikely that U.S. forces will fight the next war without heavy reliance on air forces. Yet, the utility of air forces in small wars is questionable. Those losing small wars despite air superiority include Chiang Kai-Shek, France in Indochina, Batista in Cuba, Somoza in Nicaragua, and the United States in Vietnam. Air forces and other high-tech systems present not only serious moral problems; they may also be ineffective, since they optimize combat power, not political or ethical sensitivity.

A second source of moral problems deriving from the American conventional approach to war is that we "make our allies in our own image." By dominating the local military and political situation, U.S. forces in the past have set the tone for allied forces' doctrine and force structure. In Vietnam, we created a South Vietnamese army very like our own, which then proved even less effective against the enemy than ours. Rather than assisting other forces, we tend to reform them in ways counterproductive to effective small war operations, creating infantry battalions, armored regiments and fighter squadrons. Such organization, which we do best, may clash not only with the needs of the conflict but with societal values and structure as well.

A third source is found in traditional resistance to special operations forces, which have perennially been on the short end of the force structure stick. Basically missing in active duty force structure are the vital PSYOPS, civil affairs, judge advocate general, public affairs, military police, and medical units. Among these units lie doctrinal responsibility for dealing with noncombatants, assessing public opinion, legal constraints on military actions, anti- and counterterrorism, physical security, and political expertise. Active duty commanders rarely train with such units, ensuring that these functions will not be well integrated with combat operations in the next small war. Even with the recent renewal of interest in special operations forces, the emphasis is on beefing up glamorous combat units such as special forces and Seals, and even those have been forced occasionally to tie their survival to a bureaucratic "deal," such as Army special forces taking on a conventional

NATO mission, against their basic doctrinal sense. On a larger scale, the Army's debate over doctrine for its Light Infantry Division shows the "NATO school" developing conventional rear-area missions for a force conceived as a limited war contingency unit.

The U.S. commander is trained to issue mission-type orders to maximize subordinates' initiative, intelligence, and experience, but general, mission-type orders are a dangerous way to control a unit whose every tendency is to use massive firepower to achieve purely military objectives while preserving American lives. Military operations in small wars may require the utmost clarity and sensitivity, which can be enhanced by careful command guidance. The frustration of seeking an elusive, quasi-military enemy, ambiguous orders, and tactical isolation can have tragic, immoral, and strategically disastrous consequences. One (of many) faults in the leadership and operational control that resulted in the My Lai tragedy was that Lieutenant Calley's orders were vague enough that he could interpret them as an order to murder; if his orders had *specifically forbidden* deliberate noncombatant/detainee casualties, the massacre probably would not have occurred. Military discipline and obedience in the chain of command ensure that restraint can be "dialed in" to an operation via specific orders.

The grand strategies of both the Korean and Vietnam wars were carefully limited by U.S. political leaders. Strict geographical restrictions, presidential control of some warfighting methods, continual search for negotiations, and slow, gradual escalation were the result. These civilian "limits" contrasted strongly with the military's time-honored tactics and strategies derived from conventional unlimited war: an apolitical approach of search-and-destroy, tactical bombing, and heavy artillery use. These devastated both countries (particularly Korea), resulting in unacceptable collateral damage. Thus, a pattern may be discerned, wherein U.S. small wars are limited in regional, political, and budgetary terms, but are waged by U.S. forces using strategies and tactics designed for major unlimited wars. Certainly, the frustrating limits of the Korean and Vietnam conflicts will be present in future limited wars. The U.S. military must prepare alternatives to its usual massive-firepower doctrines and force structures to operate effectively under such constraints. Proud traditions of honor and service cannot automatically correct military doctrine out of tune with the strategic requirements of much of modern war.

THE U.S. MILITARY AND SMALL WARS: ETHICAL TRAINING

As we have seen, there are moral dimensions to the lack of preparation for small wars evident in the U.S. military. However, the moral problems run much deeper, for our units today do not prepare well for the hard issues of morality in any war. All war presents American soldiers with ambiguous and emotional questions of how to fight cleanly, questions of great import to the armed forces of a liberal democracy with Western values. Yet American military training deemphasizes moral problems and relies on the unsatisfactory medium of the law of war to "solve" moral dilemmas.

A distinguished British officer wrote that the best moral climate for a soldier of a free society at war is when he has "a quiet yet active conscience."[9] That is, he is aware of the moral issues he faces (a particularly crucial requirement for limited war), yet he is satisfied with the moral latitude of his choices and moral responsibility of his leaders. This is not to argue that his hands, or his leaders' hands, are never dirty; small wars are in some ways necessarily "dirty." But the soldier in a free society, maintaining his own discipline and self-esteem, can do so only when leaders make him aware of the problems he will face, the choices he will have to make, possible consequences of the choices, and why and for how long he will face the difficult situation.

The U.S. forces are not oriented in moral challenges for several reasons. First, in training a large force for relatively short-term usefulness in a conventional mission, our training base concentrates on training volunteers in basic military and technical skills. Professional officers and NCOs spend the vast majority of their training time learning to manage the technology and administration of the services. There is no time or money to prepare conventional units for the special moral rigors of small wars. For service men and women below the rank of major (0-4), there is virtually no exposure to subjects that would prepare them for Third World political, ethnic, tribal and religious issues; the rationale for restrained firepower; the news media's role in war; domestic U.S. political-military relations; and effective allied relations. Selected O-4s and above may receive some such education at war colleges, but their professional orientation is set by that time and none of their subordinates is prepared to implement new ideas they may develop.

The morality of war in military training and education systems tends to be treated as a relatively minor adjunct to war preparation. A few hours of basic training for enlisted soldiers, several classroom discussions with a chaplain for advanced course officers, a yearly one-hour training requirement on the law of land warfare, and a total absence of moral issues from CPX and FTX characterize Army preparation for morality in war.

We rely heavily on the codified law of land warfare to provide guidance in fighting cleanly, but the approach, although logical, is fraught with peril. A "legal" approach to war and morality fails to deal with the ambiguities of a modern limited war. The U.S. Army's FM 27-10 is typical of the legal approach, labeling as a "war crime" *any* violation of the law of land warfare, thus presenting a black-and-white, unambiguous list of rules written in answer to World War II moral problems.[10] This approach trivializes the term "war crime" by failing to judge the seriousness of the act, and it ignores the fact that in a small war the soldier may not clearly see a right way to act. A legalistic approach does not treat the causes of immoral acts, but only defines some of them and establishes punishment rationale for clear, wanton criminal acts. Many of the morally questioned (and questionable) acts of U.S. forces in recent wars (strategic bombing, napalm, free-fire zones) probably were legal and certainly seemed so to those who ordered or performed them. Reliance on law cannot produce morally sound strategy in small wars; it will only give critics of unsound strategy hooks on which to hang their outrage.

Restraint and moral sensitivity in war are determined by doctrine, force structure, and training for understanding, cohesion, discipline, and effectiveness in the murky atmosphere of limited war.[11] Training a soldier to participate in the D-Day landings requires different (and less) moral sensitivity training than preparing a soldier to perform counterterrorist operations in Lebanon.

It is tragic to note that the U.S. Army, at least, has not used its greatest resource in this area, the thousands of officers and NCOs who faced the moral dilemmas of the Vietnam conflict. There is little evidence that the Army did more than turn away from that painful experience; certainly little attempt was made to pass on formally, or informally, the moral lessons of that war to those who did not serve in it.

INTERNATIONAL LAW AND SMALL WARS

International law cannot be relied upon to prepare us for the moral problems of small wars.[12] Although the International Law of War codified some of the Just War tradition for U.S. forces in such manuals as *The Law of Land Warfare* (FM 27-10), these are necessarily incomplete interpretations of the tradition. They represent the inadequate compromise of political settlement.

International laws of war treat the problems of the last war. Thus, nineteenth-century laws dealt with protecting casualties after battle and preserving prisoners' lives. Twentieth-century laws after World War II moved from such *jus in bello* concerns to the harder *jus ad bellum* issue of "aggressive war" (as practiced by Germany and Japan) affirming the legitimacy of "resistance fighters" in aggressively occupied territory. Developing a current consensus among nations has become more difficult, as issues of geopolitical force, sovereignty, and neocolonialism have emerged, dominating the simpler nineteenth-century humanitarian *jus in bello* issues.

The latest Geneva meetings (1974-77) on the laws of war considered without success aspects of modern war—the absent formal declaration, unclear boundaries, and combatant/noncombatant ambiguity. The protocols that emerged are useless to all since they fail to address any of the hard issues and are filled with the politically inflammatory rhetoric of some of the numerous Third World states participating.

The moral and legal questions of small wars are many. For example, who has legitimate authority to wage war in an age of guerrilla war? At what stage in a guerrilla war or revolution does the incumbent government lose its legitimacy? Given the permeation of some military doctrine by Marxism-Leninism and other political ideology, should laws for prisoner treatment be modified? How should combatants be defined and identified, and, with noncombatant distinctions blurred, do we need laws to protect uniformed, conventional soldiers from civilians?

These questions are too hard for the debates of international conferences to solve in time to help U.S. strategy for the next war. As military leaders, we must prepare our own "law" to ensure compliance with American and international concepts of Just War and justice in war.

MORAL STRATEGY AND TERRORISM

For all of its apparently aimless brutality, terrorism is usually carefully planned for precise political, economic, moral, or psychological effects. The terrorist may be a criminal, and Western societies must and should treat him so for moral, tactical, and jurisdictional reasons. But he is also a soldier, albeit an immoral one. Since his acts of violence are geared to political ends, they are military acts of a particularly dirty, indiscriminate kind.

Understanding the two types of terrorism points out different moral problems for U.S. forces.[13] First, in "small war" terrorism, encountered within a regional small war, both guerrillas and regime forces are capable of using violence against noncombatants for their purposes. Guerrillas seek to disrupt government control, demonstrate governmental weakness, and coerce the population through fear. Governmental forces may use terror to punish guerrilla sympathizers, gather information, or coerce.

Guerrilla terror is relatively rare in insurgency, for the guerrilla relies on population support for protection, food, and moral support. The insurgent may use an indirect terror tactic by fighting to deliberately draw a powerful military attack that kills or wounds noncombatants. He then uses media coverage of the brutality of the regime to reaffirm his role as protector of the people. In Vietnam, the Vietcong used this tactic well, fueling the fires of American public outrage. However, Vietcong guerrillas also systematically murdered and tortured widely, resulting in tens of thousands of noncombatant deaths over the years of the conflict. Although their brutality helps explain the decided lack of public support for the Communists during the Tet offensive, the tactic probably represents Marxist-Leninist standing operating procedure. The Vietcong reaped the benefits of destroying the government infrastructure in the countryside and frightening people away from government cooperation, and the police state they planned is now based on similar coercion and fear.

The guerrilla holds strategic moral cards as well. His secrecy and weakness keep his terror underground. Regime-sponsored terror is more difficult to hide and may be counterproductive in terms of demonstrating government protection for citizens. More important, no government that can be shown to use terror, torture, or violent reprisals will maintain American political support. The U.S. forces cannot fight effectively with allied units that practice terror tactics; public support will dry up. Our units may also be corrupted, as some were in Vietnam. Given that many regimes practice violent coercion and that some are expected to do so by their citizens, this constraint presents enormous obstacles for practical U.S. military intervention.

Urban terrorism differs from small war terrorism in key ways, and it is urban terror that American policy makers and strategists grapple with today. It is international in scope, often directed at unsuspecting people far from any war zone, often organized or supported by sponsoring regimes that are not at war, and often performed by professional terrorists formed into loose international networks. It is still war, violence for political ends, but while U.S. forces involved in a small war probably will face terror tactics and be forced to respond, urban terrorism presents a different problem. The U.S. military forces are not engaged, and military solutions generally are not applicable. National police forces are better trained and equipped to counter such widespread terrorism. Where urban terrorists threaten free societies, extensive use of military forces is impossible and actually would signify a major terrorist victory, as civil rights were diminished and public fear heightened.

It is possible that in attacking the sponsoring state (where one can be publicly identified), U.S. forces may have a role in counterterrorism, but the "jury is still out." President Reagan's use of air force and naval airpower against Libya avoided some of the pitfalls of American moral attitudes towards war. It was "just," following closely on Libyan-sponsored terrorist attacks when American outrage was strong, and it was brief and "victorious," avoiding public impatience while providing a "solution." However, as in many small war operations, the noncombatant deaths and injury seriously detracted from the perceived justice of the attack. Although we sought to attack "purely military targets," there may be none in such conflicts. A second problem in using U.S. forces against urban terrorists or sponsoring states is the legitimacy thus conferred upon the enemy. Our policy assumes the terrorist is a despicable criminal, yet using U.S. armed forces brings the terrorist into international geopolitics, legitimizing his political rhetoric, often building up indigenous public support for his cause. Again, Ghadaffi is an excellent example.

The U.S. strategists and trainers must view small war terrorism as a tactic within the context of some wars, and U.S. forces and allies must avoid such tactics and set a double standard in which the enemy's use of terror is not answered in kind. Otherwise, American support will fail. Urban terrorism, primarily a police responsibility, may be amenable to retaliatory strikes against sponsoring states; however, the moral and political risks of such action are high.

In summary, the U.S. military must do three things to deal with the moral problems certain to be faced in the next small war. First, the United States must study the problem—study small wars in terms of moral values and perspectives and look for patterns in the interaction of the Western Just War tradition and other cultures. The United States must overcome its tendency to forget old lessons and must study its past small wars, especially drawing on the dwindling numbers of active-duty Vietnam veterans to teach the moral lessons of Vietnam.

Secondly, the U.S. military must deal with the issue of civil-military relations, by advising the president and his Cabinet of the possible moral consequences of inserting U.S. forces and must advise caution in insertion of conventional forces, emphasizing using noncombatant special operations forces for training and direct assistance to allied forces. And, the U.S. military must continue to improve relations with the media so that before a war they understand the military and its force structure and operations.

Third and finally, the U.S. military must begin to reorient forces to be able to fight with restraint and social and political sensitivity. Expensive, difficult solutions, such as creating a Special Operations Command or drastically restructuring the active-reserve force mix are not practical. Rather, the military must continue to develop practical low-intensity doctrine, concentrating on the nature of such war and the kind of enemy to be faced.

The professional military must revamp military education and training. Officers, from the beginning of their careers, must receive politico-military orientation, learning how they fit into American political institutions and how use of armed force affects the domestic and international environment. Officers must be trained to command conventional forces in dirty small wars. Officer education must include restraining firepower, indigenous issues and languages, political sensitivity, and sustaining high morale, discipline, and cohesion under the extended pressure of public criticism, cultural disjunction, political restraint and sporadic casualties. Enlisted training should emphasize how to fight with restraint (and why it is important) and how to maintain morale, discipline, and cohesion in small wars.

The U.S. military members, planners, strategists, and leaders face the prospect of numerous small wars and limited conflicts over the remainder of this century and into the next. A major component of the U.S. strategic planning for these wars must involve the moral problems faced in them. We can do no greater service to ourselves, our armed forces, our troops, and the American public than to prepare to face these moral issues.

NOTES

1. Major sources for the discussion about the so-called moral "advantage" of guerrillas included William V. O'Brien, *The Conduct of Just and Limited War* (New York: Praeger, 1983); Paul Ramsey, *The Just War* (New York: Charles Scribner's Sons, 1983); and Guenter Lewy, *America in Vietnam* (New York: Oxford University Press, 1978).

2. Several sources can provide further insight into this issue. William V. O'Brien, in *The Conduct of Just and Limited War* (New York: Praeger, 1983), argued that U.S. forces must set their own moral standards in a dirty war. He also discussed in some depth the existence and implication of the "sliding scale" of moral judgment. Guenter Lewy, in *America in Vietnam* (New York: Oxford University Press, 1978), provided a lengthy, insightful analysis of the "war crimes industry" that exaggerated and even manufactured U.S. "war crimes" in Vietnam. Paul Ramsey, in *The Just War* (New York: Charles Scribner's Sons, 1968), courageously took on the Vietnam antiwar lobby in discussing the illogic of some of their criticism and the dangerous separation of the U.S. military from its constituency that resulted.

3. William V. O'Brien, *The Conduct of Just and Limited War* (New York: Praeger, 1983), discussed the extensive American attempts to fight a just war in Vietnam, both in *jus ad bellum* (negotiations and truces) and *jus in bello* (rules of engagement, command warnings, etc.).

4. Robert W. Tucker, in *The Just War* (Baltimore: The Johns Hopkins Press, 1960), condemns even before the Vietnam war the tendency of U.S. forces to respect the "humanity" of only U.S. soldiers, using "military necessity" to justify massive collateral damage.

5. Comprehensive and remarkably current and valuable analysis of American civil-military relations and military professionalism can be found in Morris Janowitz, *The Professional Sol-*

SMALL WARS AND MORALLY SOUND STRATEGY

dier: *A Social and Political Portrait* (New York: Free Press, 1960; reprint ed. with new prologue by the author, New York: Free Press, 1971) and Samuel P. Huntington, *The Soldier and the State: The Theory and Politics of Civil-Military Relations* (Cambridge, MA: Harvard University Press, 1957). Despite their age, these studies represent the best source for studying origins of current professional standards, doctrine and traditions. All officers should read them.

6. Basic sources for the dangers of "management" in the armed services include: Douglas Kinnard, *The War Managers* (Hanover, NH: University Press of New England, 1977), and Richard A. Gabriel and Paul L. Savage, *Crisis in Command: Mismanagement in the Army* (New York: Hill and Wang, 1978).

7. The U.S. Army published a comprehensive doctrinal manual which is worth studying: DA, Training and Doctrine Command (TRADOC) Pamphlet 525-44, *U.S. Army Operational Concept for Low-Intensity Conflict*, (Fort Monroe, VA: Oct 18, 1985).

8. The problem of applying massive conventional power to limited war has many aspects. Michael Walzer, in *Just and Unjust War* (New York: Basic Books, 1977), discussed from a moral philosophy point of view the inability of U.S. forces in Vietnam to respect the scope and character of the war. Morris Janowitz, in *The Professional Soldier* (New York: Free Press, 1971), analyzed the dialogue between strategic "absolutists" and "pragmatists" in the U.S. military profession, and the implications for limited war. Janowitz also discussed the tendency of U.S. forces to recreate their own image in military assistance programs, and their tendency to handle local political and social issues with the tactical organization of U.S. field armies. Robert E. Osgood, in *Limited War Revisited* (Boulder, CO: Westview, 1979), discussed the consequences of placing civilian and political limitations on U.S. conventional forces, and the probability that future limited wars will present similar problems. An excellent analysis of matching U.S. forces to special operations and limited conflict can be found in: Allen Dodson, ed., *The Role of Airpower in Low Intensity Conflict: Proceedings from the Ninth Air University Airpower Symposium* (Maxwell AFB, AL: Air War College, 1985).

9. Sir James Glover, "A Soldier and His Conscience," *Parameters*, September 1983, pp. 53-58.

10. U.S. Department of the Army, *The Law of Land Warfare*, FM 27-10, July 1956, p. 178. Review of this manual will reveal its unsuitability for preparing our units for small, dirty wars.

11. For an excellent discussion of the inadequacy of explicit legal prescriptions in limiting belligerent behavior, see William V. O'Brien, *The Conduct of Just and Limited War* (New York: Praeger, 1983).

12. Clausewitz seemed to argue that law and custom are of no value in mitigating the effects of war (see Carl von Clausewitz, *On War*, Princeton, NJ: Princeton University Press, 1976, p. 75), but closer reading of the text reveals that his caveat applied to his theory of "pure war," that *actual* war is bounded and controlled by the standards and customs of the societies waging it. Excellent discussions of the history and current irrelevance of modern international law to modern warfare are found in: Geoffrey Best, *Humanity in Warfare* (New York: Columbia University Press, 1980) and Keith Suter, *An International Law of Guerrilla Warfare* (New York: St. Martin's Press, 1984).

13. The following authors analyze various aspects of small war terrorism: Its political and military character; Barrie Paskins and Michael Dockrill, *The Ethics of War* (Minneapolis: University of Minnesota Press, 1979). The nature of guerrilla terrorism, its rarity and manipulative character; Robert L. Phillips, *War and Justice* (Norman: University of Oklahoma Press, 1984). The advisability of counterguerrilla forces accepting a moral "double standard"; William V. O'Brien, *The Conduct of Just and Limited War* (New York, Praeger, 1983). Vietcong terrorism: Guenter Lewy, *America in Vietnam* (New York: Oxford University Press, 1978). The necessity to retaliate with military attacks against today's national "sponsors" of international terrorism; Alvin Bernstein, "Iran's Low-Intensity War Against the United States." Unpublished paper, U.S. Naval War College, Newport, R.I.: 1985. The danger of conferring legitimacy on the terrorist by fighting him with military forces: Christopher Dobson and Ronald Payne, *Counterattack: The West's Battle Against the Terrorists* (New York: Facts on File, 1982), p. 2.

°⊚)| |(℮°

WOMEN IN COMBAT ROLES?

PAUL CHRISTOPHER
Major, US Army

Major Christopher considers several of the traditional arguments against combat assignments for women: the average woman has less physical strength than the average man; the nurturing instinct of women will prevent them from making objective battlefield decisions; men will be overly protective of women in their combat units; sexual involvements will degrade unit cohesion. Major Christopher finds all of these arguments seriously defective, and he concludes there is "no good reason to exclude females from filling combat roles in our armed forces."

Women in the armed forces continue to be the subject of considerable debate, with every change made by one of the services in the jobs open to women becoming another news item met with both praise and condemnation. Considering the many changes made in the last few years, along with the current trend, it seems that we are gradually achieving a completely integrated force. Still, the questioning of whether or not women should be placed in combat units remains extremely controversial.

Should there be certain limits on the integration of women into the armed forces? What, if any, limitations should be placed on the use of females in military jobs based on either (a) physical, psychological, or emotional differences; (b) social conventions; or (c) economic considerations. It seems to me that the burden of justification should be on those that would exclude women from certain jobs, rather than on those who advocate total equality.

In the arguments that advocate limited use of females in combat roles based on their physical capabilities, there are a number of variations, yet all basically asserting the same key point, which can be characterized as follows:

Argument A.

A1. If certain people are physically less capable, then there should be some restrictions placed on their assignment to certain military jobs.

A2. The average woman is physically less capable than the average man.

Conclusion: There should be some restrictions placed on the assignment of women to certain military jobs.

At first glance this argument might seem plausible. There is, however, a bit of sleight-of-hand that leads us to a false conclusion. To illustrate, consider the following similarly structured argument (assume the premises are true):

Argument B.

B1. If someone has children, then that person should be required to maintain at least $50,000 in life insurance until the children reach the age of eighteen.

B2. The average plumber in New Jersey has 1.26 children below the age of eighteen.

Conclusion: All plumbers in New Jersey should be required to maintain at least $50,000 in life insurance.

Argument B employs the same sleight-of-hand used in *Argument A*. The error lies in the assumption that there is such a thing as an "average plumber." An average anything, like a Platonic Form, enjoys only a conceptual, rather than a physical, existence. This is much more obvious to us in *Argument B* because people do not have fractions of children, and it is equally apparent that there are likely to be some plumbers in New Jersey who do not have any children. It would, therefore, be an error to require plumbers with no children to abide by the conclusion of this invalid argument. Similarly just as what is true about the average plumber may not be true about any individual plumber, what is true of the average female might not be true of most females, and certainly is not true of all of them. Specifically, then, the fallacy in *Argument A* lies in taking what may be true about the average female and concluding that this same quality is true of all females. We must, therefore, reject *Argument A*.

Possibly, one could attempt to modify the argument so that the conclusion is supported by the premises:

Argument C.

C1. Most women do not meet the minimum physical standards for military service in combat units.

C2. If *most* women do not meet the minimum standards for military service in combat units, then *all* women should be excluded from service in combat units.

Conclusion: All women should be excluded from military service in combat units.

Although while C1 and C2 support the conclusion, the former seems at least questionable, and the latter is patently false. Regarding C1, there is not, at least to common knowledge, a definitive minimum standard of physical performance specific to combat units. If a standard were one to be developed, there would be a significant difference in the percentages of men and women who could attain it. More important, however, is the illogical nature of C2, concluding that because some women are not physically qualified for certain positions that no women should be permitted in those positions. In fact, although it may be perfectly reasonable to restrict assignments to combat units based on physical standards, it is completely unreasonable and discriminatory to apply those standards only to one particular group. If physical standards are to provide a basis for assignment to combat units, they must be applied equally to both sexes. One must, therefore, reject those arguments that seek to exclude women from combat roles based on an alleged physical difference.

A second common objection to employing women in combat units rests on an alleged emotional/psychological disparity between men and women. Proponents of this view maintain that women are more nurturing or "motherly" than men are, and that this characteristic will interfere with their ability to "place the mission before the men" when the situation calls for it. Specifically, women are unsuitable for leadership positions in combat because of an inability to make tough battlefield decisions objectively. This argument might be constructed as follows:

Argument D.

D1. If certain persons are deficient in their ability to make objective decisions regarding matters of life and death, then those persons should be excluded from military positions which are likely to require such decisions (i.e., combat positions).

D2. Women, in virtue of their innate, biological disposition to nurture, will have a more difficult time with these life and death decisions than will men.

Conclusion: Women should be excluded from those military positions (combat specialties) where they are likely to be faced with life and death decisions.

At first glance this argument seems open to the same objection as *Argument C*: that is, simply exclude both the men and the women who lack the requisite emotional traits from those specific positions for which they are not suited. This response, however, is not effective because proponents of *Argument D* can reply that unlike with physical ability, which is readily measured, no feasible tool exists for measuring emotional capability. Because the ability cannot be measured and because it is known to be a characteristically feminine quality, there is no choice but to exclude females as a group.

The first premise in this argument appears incontestable, leaving D2 as the focus of attention, but two questions must be answered in the affirmative to accept D2. First, is it true that women are innately more nurturing than men; second, if so, will this adversely interfere with their ability to make objective decisions on the battlefield? Let's examine each in turn.

The first flawed aspect of the "more nurturing" question is that the argument is not adequate, stating simply women are more nurturing than men; the reason for their being so must be natural rather than social. For example, if women are required by the conventions of a particular culture to behave in a certain way, then one can't use the fact that they behave in that way as an argument to prove that they should behave in that way. This leaves a proposition that is much more difficult to defend: that is, women are by their very nature more nurturing than men. Moreover, those who would defend this view must argue that women are not only more nurturing in a particular role or relationship, such as that of mother and her child but are more nurturing in other associations as well (for example, in the work place). Such associations must be obviously either one of two types: with a member of the opposite sex (male/female) or with a member of the same sex (female/female).

Restating the premise under examination, it is affirmed that women are innately more nurturing than men in their relationships with members of the same sex and/or in their relationships with members of the opposite sex. To examine the truth of this contention, considering homogeneous relationships first, it seems highly questionable to suppose that the relationships that women develop with other women are any stronger or more nurturing than the relationships that men develop with other men. In fact, it seems more reasonable to believe that the bonds of friendship that develop between members of the same sex are no different for women than they are for men. There is no reason to believe that the female "bonding" that occurs through normal association is any stronger than the male bonding that is said to occur. And even if some instances of exceptionally strong ties between females were documented, it is not reasonable to suppose that such relationships are based on some innate disposition. Indeed, to maintain that women are more nurturing than men, the argument must encompass only their relationships with the opposite sex. However, even this reduced proposition seems to yield the very opposite of what we would suppose. When we consider most male/female relationships, such as husband/ wife or girlfriend/boyfriend, it is the man—not the woman—that is usually considered to be the more protective and nurturing! In fact, this contention that men are more protective of women than they are of other men forms the basis for a separate argument on why women should be excluded from combat roles.

Although it is reasonable to accept that some women might be more nurturing in particular relationships, one must also accept that the same is undoubtedly true of some men. One could conclude, therefore, that women are not naturally disposed to be more nurturing than men are in their relationships with others of the same or opposite sex.

These discussions leave no choice but to reject the idea that women have an innate biological disposition to nurture that extends beyond their relationship with their children. At a minimum, the argument that women so exceed men in an innate disposition to indiscriminately nurture others as to render them deficient in decisionmaking ability is one that is clearly untenable. Premise D2 and *Argument D* must therefore be rejected.

Another tack that is sometimes taken by those who would exclude women from combat roles argues that although they should be treated equally, existing social conventions will not permit it. Those who take this position hold that men are simply not prepared to treat male and female soldiers equally; in fact, men will invariably be more protective (nurturing) of women because of the traditional male familial role. This propensity of males to be protective of women may impede the ability of many males in making rational, objective, battlefield decisions. Simply put, at least until our social conventions change, women will have to be satisfied with roles in the armed forces that reflect those conventions— even if they are wrong. This argument might be formalized as follows.

Argument E.

E1. If the male population from which the military strength is drawn is not prepared to treat women equally (because of social conventions), then women must not be permitted into jobs where such unequal treatment might endanger lives (i.e., combat roles).

E2. The U.S. male population is not prepared to treat women equally.

Conclusion: Women should be excluded from combat roles.

A number of problems accompany this argument. First, one might take issue with E2 and argue that the phrase "male population" is only a conceptual entity (much like the plumber with 1.26 children), at least insofar as it can be said to hold beliefs. Even if large numbers of males in the United States are so indiscriminately protective of females as to render them incapable of treating men and women equally, for a fact not all are. But as serious as this criticism of *Argument E* is, there is an even more serious one, illustrated by substituting racial considerations for those of sex:

E1. If the population from which the military is drawn is not prepared to treat blacks (or any race or religious group) equally, then blacks (or all members of that particular group) should be excluded from those jobs where unequal treatment might endanger lives.

This line of reasoning attempts to separate the military services from the society that they represent. Military institutions do not merely reflect society; they are an important part of it. Military leaders should not allow themselves to be stonewalled by those who refuse to modify behavior when they recognize such behavior to be immoral.

If members of the armed forces are perpetuating prejudicial actions against a group of people, it is the responsibility of all enlightened persons to do what they can to modify such behavior. An example will help clarify this point. There was deep and widespread resistance to the racial integration of military units when it was first directed by President Truman following World War II. In fact, units were still largely segregated at the beginning of the Korean conflict. Today, however, no one would dispute that such action (that is, the segregation of units) was blatantly wrong even though we acknowledge that it had widespread support. We are simply not prepared to accept false beliefs as an adequate justification for perpetuating social prejudices or discriminatory actions. As a nation we have come to this conclusion, at least insofar as it pertains to issues of racial prejudice, and hence, we readily reject premise E1. But the argument supporting sexual discrimination similarly depends on a willingness to perpetuate discrimination based on a belief we acknowledge to be false. We must also recognize that we cannot condone discriminatory sexual practices based on beliefs that have no factual or substantive basis and that we acknowledge to be false—even if such beliefs are widely held by a certain unenlightened segment of the population. Clearly, the armed forces must provide positive leadership in matters of social change—at least internally—the same way they did with the issue of racial integration. Even if one accepts the dubious claim that most U.S. males are unable to be objective in decisions involving both men and women, one cannot reasonably advocate that the armed services acquiesce in what constitutes prejudicial behavior, as E2 would require. *Argument E must be rejected.*

Another socially based argument that one might offer as justification for excluding women from combat roles focuses on the likelihood of sexual involvement. Proponents of this position argue that when men and women live and work together for extended periods (for example, battlefield scenarios), it is inevitable that some will become sexually involved. Sexual involvement among team members, they add, may lead to jealousy, animosity or even hatred— emotions that severely detract from combat readiness and that cannot be tolerated in combat units. One might construct this argument in this way:

Argument F.

F1. If men and women live and work together (as is required by members of combat units), some will inevitably become sexually involved.

F2. If some members of a unit become sexually involved, it is likely to cause jealousy, animosity, or hatred among unit members.

F3. If a combat unit experiences jealousy, animosity, or hatred among unit members, then it will suffer a degradation of unit cohesion and effectiveness.

F4. Anything which is likely to cause a degradation in effectiveness or cohesion should be avoided.

Conclusion: Women should be excluded from combat units.

On the surface, this seems to be a powerful argument. The point of contention is premise F2. Is it true that in those organizations where members are involved sexually, that this involvement results in increased animosity? Some commentators don't think so, and some believe that there are numerous counterexamples that demonstrate the falsity of this claim.

The Corps of Cadets at the United States Military Academy lives and works together in a restricted environment; the Corps is comprised of approximately 10 percent women. If F2 were true, then it is likely that the effects it predicts in heterogeneous groups would be magnified in organizations where there exists increased competition for sexual favors. We find, however, that is not the case at West Point, or any of the other military service academies. In fact, while many "naysayers" opposed the initial admission of women to the military academies based on similar arguments, time has shown them to be groundless. Likewise, those combat support units that have integrated women into their force have not suffered an increase in interpersonal animosities. And indeed, the great majority of the workplaces in America employ both men and women in a common work environment without suffering the negative emotions predicted by F2. Governmental organizations such as police departments and fire departments all hire both male and female qualified applicants, apparently without any degradation in effectiveness. Instead of women loosening the bonds of camaraderie between workers, they have themselves become an important part of the social infrastructure. Based on such examples there is no reason whatsoever to suppose that it will be any different in military combat units. Hence, F2 and *Argument F* must be rejected.

An argument similar to that of *Argument E* can also examine the view that women must be excluded from combat roles because of economic considerations. This argument is similar to *Argument E* in that proponents of this view concede that although it would be preferable to treat men and women equally, it is simply not practical due to some special considerations, in this case, economic factors. In this age of budget cuts and reduced military sending, they argue, it is not feasible to incur the enormous expenses associated with catering to a group of biologically different individuals. One might formalize the argument this way:

Argument G.

G1. If excluding a certain group of biologically different individuals from specific military specialties would save substantial sums of money, then it is reasonable to so exclude them.

G2. Excluding women from combat roles would save a substantial amount of money.

Conclusion: It is reasonable to exclude women from combat roles based on economic considerations.

Obviously, the premise that is questionable in this argument is G2. Proponents of this position cannot be referring to increased expenses that might be incurred because of differences in physical strength between men and women because that argument has been shown to be unsound in *Argument C.* In fact, who can imagine precisely what economic savings are being referred to in G2? Indeed, it seems more reasonable to argue that the inclusion of women in the recruiting pool would *save money.* Some correlation probably exists between the amount of money spent on recruiting and the numbers of prospective recruits from which to draw. It seems that with the

addition of females to this group—a considerable
increase indeed—that the armed forces would be
able to either raise the standards for acceptance
(thereby improving the quality of the force), reduce
the money spent on the recruiting effort, or do both.
As the available recruiting pool is reduced with the
changing national demographics, should combat
units accept substandard fills or even empty positions, rather than accepting women? No matter how
one answers this question, the premise that it is not
economically sound to admit women to combat jobs
seems patently false.

Without a good reason to exclude females from
filling combat roles in our armed forces, those who
oppose such a change based on intuition, tradition,
or a delusion regarding the masculine role should
forgo this view—in the face of rational analysis. The
armed forces should stop discriminatory hiring practices for combat positions.

INDEX

INDEX

INDEX

Ghadaffi, Muammar, 161, 218
Generals, passed over for
promotion, 47
Geneva Conventions, 145, 151,
161–62 n.1, 163 n.7
German High Command
limits of loyalty, 89
Operation Valkyrie, 57–60,
62
Grenada rescue operations, 153,
156, 192
Guderian, Heinz, 58, 66, 68, 72
n.25
Guerrillas
collateral damage and
atrocities, 197
legitimacy of, 214
manipulation of public
opinion, 197
moral advantage of, 195–96,
198
Shining Path movement, 165
n.13
terrorism by, 215–16
Gulf of Sidra incident, 153

Hackett, John, 19
Hart, Liddell, 68
Hastings Center, 138
Health care. See also Physicians,
military
fiscal constraints on, 106–7
Heinl, Colonel, 31
Helms, Richard, 130
Heusinger, Adolf, 58, 66, 69–70
Hitler, Adolf
assassination attempt, see
Operation Valkyrie
officer's sworn obligations to,
20, 65
public support of, 66
Homosexuality/bisexuality, 104

Honor, and intelligence
collection, 121
Human immunodeficiency virus
infection, 104
Human rights, and obedience,
70
Hume, David, 21–23, 26
Hundert, E.M., 103
Huntington, Samuel P., 11
Hurlburt Field, 154

Immigration and Naturalization
Act, 19
Incendiary bombing and napalm
use, 200, 212
Institutions
just nature of, 66, 67, 70
U.S. military problems in
small wars, 202–10
Instruction/teaching in ethics.
See also Law of War
training
barriers to, 205–6
causes of ethical dilemmas,
142
competence and, 137, 139–40,
141
consultation/discussion in,
142–43
controversial nature of ethics
and, 137, 139
expectations in, 141–42
goal clarification, 138–39, 141
indifference and resistance to,
135, 136–40
in intelligence operations,
115–16, 131–32
methods and techniques,
143–44
practical problems in, 135–36,
143
in professions, 136–37
purposes of, 140–41

INDEX

INDEX

INDEX

THE EDITORS

James C. Gaston has extensive experience as a teacher of both English (at the U.S. Air Force Academy) and national security policy (at the Industrial College of the Armed Forces). As an editor, he has combined these perspectives to benefit a wide range of studies in national security. Recently he has dealt with domestic concerns as diverse as defense nuclear wastes, economic conditions in Indonesia and Melanesia, and shifting political alignments in Sub-Saharan Africa.

Janis Bren Hietala is the senior Writer-Editor with the Research Directorate, a division of the Institute for National Strategic Studies at National Defense University. She has edited numerous books on national defense for the NDU Press. Previously, she edited Army regulations, circulars, and pamphlets as a part of Army's clear writing program. Ms. Hietala is a graduate of the University of Minnesota.

☆ U.S. GOVERNMENT PRINTING OFFICE: 1993 282-306/40013

For sale by U. S. Government Printing Office
Superintendent of Documents, Mail Stop: SSOP
Washington, DC. 20402-9328
ISBN 0-16-035907-4